4/21

BIBLICAL MEDITATIONS FOR LENT

ALSO BY CARROLL STUHLMUELLER:

Biblical Meditations for the Easter Season
Biblical Meditations for Advent
    and the Christmas Season
Biblical Meditations for Ordinary Time
    (Weeks 1–9)
Biblical Meditations for Ordinary Time
    (Weeks 10–22)
Biblical Meditations for Ordinary Time
    (Weeks 23–34)

Biblical Meditations
for
Lent

by

Carroll Stuhlmueller, C.P.

Introduction by
Roger Mercurio, C.P.

PAULIST PRESS
New York / Mahwah

IMPRIMI POTEST
Roger Mercurio, C.P.
Provincial, Holy Cross Province
Chicago, Illinois
September 7, 1977

Library of Congress
Catalog Card Number: 77-91366

ISBN: 0-8091-2089-5

Published by Paulist Press
997 Macarthur Blvd.
Mahwah, NJ 07430

Printed and bound in the
United States of America

CONTENTS

To
The Passionist Communities
of
Holy Cross Province
where I learn to love the
Bible and prayer

FOREWORD

These *Biblical Meditations for Lent* flow from the same kind of setting where most of the books and sections of the Bible were born and transmitted—with God's people together at prayer. The Scriptures did not emerge from the pen of scholars, nor, of course, from their electric typewriters, as they were flanked with foreign commentaries and their Hebrew and Greek lexicons. Rather, as the words of Moses and Jesus and other great leaders of biblical times were repeated by the Israelites and the early Christians, these words became prayers for help, songs for celebration, instructions for new situations. All agreed that God's holy Spirit was inspiring the evolution from individual words to community prayers, hymns and instructions. Religious leaders gave a formal stamp of approval, and the Bible continued to grow.

To study and pray the Bible today means to vibrate with the pulse and energy of the same Spirit, living then within Israel and the early Church, now sustaining our communities. With the assistance of this Holy Spirit, Bible study and Bible prayer become a joyful, encouraging and most peaceful pursuit. To open the Scriptures is to find God, as one of its writers confessed:

> *Happy* are they who observe his decrees,
>   *who seek him* with all their heart.
> I will keep your statutes;
>   do not utterly forsake me.
> *With all my heart* I seek you

let me not stray from your commands.
In the way of your decrees *I rejoice* ,
as much as in all riches.
(Ps 119:2, 8, 10, 14)

This book reflects upon the Bible as its words live within *our* community of faith. Here in the Church is where the different gifts, ministries and works are united in a living, challenging and evolving way, where the one God—Father, Son and Spirit—dwells (2 Cor 6:16; 1 Cor 12:27-30; Col 1:24). The Church is an integral part of today's world and comes to terms with its problems and crises, its hopes and frustrations through the wisdom of the Scriptures and the ancient traditions of her saints and leaders.

The meditations in this book interact with the two or three readings of each weekday and Sunday of Lent. One biblical reading casts light into the depths of the other, and from this union there is conceived a new child or life in the Spirit. This new creature stirs with wonder, hope and challenge.

This process not only unites our hearts and our times with the ancient days of the Bible but it directs each meditation of this book into our contemporary world.

First , a summary of each Bible reading is given. These quick statements are no substitute for reading the entire section in one's Bible or liturgical book. They focus upon the main ideas in the meditation to follow. On rare occasions when the Bible may be missing, these condensed statements may allow the reader to proceed more easily with the meditation.

The principal part of these meditations is always the Bible, but *the longest section* in the book is given to reflection. Here we gratefully accept the careful work of the scholars, particularly over the last forty to seventy years. Because of this scientific investigation, we are able not only to appreciate the context of the ancient Scriptures, but especially to feel the challenge of this pure thrust of the Spirit into our lives and Church today. The meaning of the Bible for us is found when the same Holy Spirit lives in ourselves as a Church at prayer.

The author of these reflections forms but one Church—really, one body of the Lord—with you, the reader, in your moment at prayer. Your reflections ought to replace the author's; your responsiveness to the Spirit will rewrite the meditations. At least, the silent reaction of all of us at prayer, sensing the Spirit joyfully or sorrowfully, with perplexity or with temptation, perhaps with no other distinctive awareness than the ecstatic "My Lord and my God!" (John 20:28), is where the mystery of God's word is experienced.

This attitude of sustained waiting upon the Lord may be aided by the short prayer at the close of each meditation, usually drawn from the responsorial psalm of that day's liturgy.

The indices at the end will direct the resources of this book to preparing Bible Services. An asterisk indicates major Scriptural references. The topical index will be useful as well for the rite of reconciliation and directed retreats.

This book grew out of several years of personal prayer during the early morning hours of Lent, with a small missal, pencil and pad of paper at hand. Each notation was intended only as a goad or directive for prayerful recollection during the rest of the day, which was usually capped with the Eucharistic liturgy. The

material would have remained just poorly written jot-
tings in all sorts of scattered notebooks, if Robert Heyer
of Paulist Press had not taken the initiative to request a
Scripture meditation book for Lent. I am happy to
re-live the initial moments of prayer in composing this
manuscript and so to have returned again to the Lord,
our God (Hos 14:2).

While the origins of this book lie in the prompting
of the Spirit and in the treasures of the Bible, this Holy
Spirit lived and breathed in my heart through the religious community of men, known as the Passionists. I
have been privileged to live for many years as a member
of this religious order, where my desire for prayer and
love of Scripture were nurtured. I am indebted to my
spiritual directors, professors, superiors and brother
religious.

The manuscript was carefully and quickly typed by
Sister Mary Eva Strasser, S.S.N.D., of the Academy of
Our Lady, Chicago. To her I extend my warm gratitude.

Carroll Stuhlmueller, C.P.
The Catholic Theological Union at Chicago

Introduction

Lent has been an intense spiritual experience for followers of Christ throughout the centuries. Christians of ancient Rome early developed impressive Lenten liturgies, centering around the stational churches. For medieval Europeans Lent was a time for prolonged prayer, severe bodily discipline and generous alms giving. Early in this century our grandparents observed Lent with frequent, even daily Mass, public devotional practices and austere fasting.

A decade ago the Second Vatican Council changed the focus of Lent to "a period of closer attention to the Word of God and more ardent prayer" (*Constitution on the Sacred Liturgy*, #109). To meet this need the Church proposed a new Lectionary of biblical readings for the Sundays and weekdays of Lent. These carefully balanced selections offer the Christian assembly a rich source for Lenten reflection.

Perhaps at times we find the table of God's Word too lavish for our tastes. Perhaps we do not allow ourselves the time to chew and absorb the Scriptures. It may be we do not wait sufficiently upon the Lord (Is 30:15), so that his word may flow through veins of our mind with new insights and through the ventricles of our heart with fervent love, a strong love enabling our hands to reach outward to all our many neighbors.

Each day during Lent the Lord invites us through his prophet:

> All who are thirsty,
>   come to the water!

You who have no money,
>   come, receive grain and eat;
Come, without paying and without cost,
>   drink wine and milk!

Why spend your money for what is not bread;
>   your wages for what fails to satisfy?
Heed me, and you shall eat well,
>   you shall delight in rich fare.
Come to me heedfully,
>   listen, that you may have life. . . .

So shall my word be
>   that goes forth from my mouth;
It shall not return to me void,
>   but shall do my will,
>   achieving the end for which I sent it.
(Is 55:1-3, 11)

Father Carroll Stuhlmueller, the author of these meditations, shares with us his own Lenten reflections on the new Lectionary. He brings to his meditations experiences of many years. As a young Passionist he absorbed the spirit of prayer bequeathed to his religious congregation by the founder, St. Paul of the Cross. Then as a student of the Old Testament and later as a dedicated biblical teacher, he has been able to combine scholarly erudition with humble faith as he tastes deeply of the bread of the Word. Through worldwide lecturing the full richess and scope of God's word became ever more impressed upon him. This word, he learned, speaks everywhere.

God's word speaks most effectively at the

Eucharistic liturgy. Here it resounds from many hearts and resonates at once the rich diversity and strong unity of God's people. Frequently within his own religious family Fr. Carroll Stuhlmueller has caught the momentum of such assemblies of prayer and shared his biblical reflections in brief homilies.

The Word we hear or share at liturgy is a Word enriched by sacrifice, memorial and communion. It is now a Word "enfleshed" in sacrament, which seeks in turn to be "enfleshed" in the lives of the community. It is a Word "sown" in the "Body of Christ" and reaching out for fruitfulness in the services and ministries of the people of God who are also the "Body of Christ."

Through the publication of these Lenten prayers Father Carroll invites many others to join him in meditating the daily Scriptures. This book is, indeed, an invitation to form community in the communion of Christ and his Word.

It has been a privilege and inspiration for me to have known Father Carroll these many years. It is an especial joy to be asked to write a brief introduction to his book on Scripture and liturgy—themes dear to me also from my own years as seminary professor of New Testament and Liturgical Studies. My happy memories even reach back to classroom days when Carroll was a student of mine!

I trust that Father Carroll has asked me to write this introduction, not because I chance to be his Provincial Superior at this particular time, but because of our long relationship as Passionist brothers and associates in biblical studies. Within this bond of friendship and faith I commend this book to a large audience. I pray that many will find Lenten nourishment as they wait upon the Word of God to speak in the Scriptures and to become enfleshed in the Sacrament of the Eucharist and of the Church.

Roger Mercurio, C.P.
Provincial Superior
Passionist Provincial Office
Chicago, Illinois

PART ONE

Weekdays of Lent

ASH WEDNESDAY TO SATURDAY

Ash Wednesday

Joel 2:12-18. A fast is proclaimed; an assembly of prayer is called. Then the Lord took pity on his people.

2 Cor 5:20-6:2. Jesus was made "sin" for our sakes, so that in him we might become the very holiness of God. What opportunity is ours *now*. Now is the day of salvation.

Matt 6:1-6, 16-18. Be on your guard against performing religious acts for people to see.

Lent summons *all of us* —the elders, the children and the infants, the priests and the ministers, even the bride and bridegroom—to "fasting and weeping and mourning." No matter how happy or innocent or secure anyone of us may be, we are summoned to an assembly of the sorrowful, the sinful and the anxious. Love and compassion should be so strong and compelling that we become a member of that family ridden with death or a great disappointment, with sickness and destitution, with guilt and serious mistakes.

"Fasting and weeping and mourning" bring tears to our worried eyes, an ache to our empty stomach, anxiety to our heart overwhelmed with grief. Members of our family—whom we love as brothers and sisters, father and mother, husband and wife—are weeping, are dying of hunger, and are convulsed with agony. We are so immersed in this, our family, that *we become* their tears, their hunger, their frustration, just as Jesus became "sin" for our sakes, so thoroughly did Jesus wrap our flesh and blood around himself (2 Cor 5:21; Rom 8:3).

During Lent we bring immediately before God the

sin, the godlessness, the death, the curse of rejection. "Perhaps he will again relent." Our God is "gracious and merciful . . . and relenting in punishment." Lent proceeds on the principle that God must show compassion at the sight of misery, even if that misery is induced wilfully by sin. Lent also carries the hope that each of us will thereby absorb something of God's gracious concern and continual desire to relent and forgive. If Lent offers us an opportunity to share the mind, heart and conscience of the sinful and the sick, it also affords us a chance to be forgiven for our refusal to forgive others, to be cured of our secret pride and bias, and to have our cold insensitivity warmed with true affection.

Our own transformation must be deeply interior and dependable for the months and years ahead. "Rend your hearts, not your garments." "Be on your guard against performing religious acts for people to see." Jesus' words in Matthew's gospel about keeping your deeds of mercy secret do not contradict the prophet Joel who sanctifies a public assembly and calls for a general period of fasting and mourning. Both Joel and Jesus summon all of us to act as a *single family* of love—to be but one family—just as Jesus became thoroughly incarnate into our human family, even to be "sin" as we are sinful! Whatever is done in a family, is done spontaneously, without show, without counting the cost and expecting a return. It is done altogether, so easily, that the left hand does not know what the right hand is doing.

> Spare, O Lord, your people,
> > and make not your heritage a reproach
> > with the nations ruling over us.

> Why should they say among the peoples,
> > "Where is their God?"

Thursday After Ash Wednesday

Deut 30:15-20. Obedience, with love, ensures life; disobedience and hatred bring death and a curse.

Luke 9:22-25. Take up one's cross daily, to follow Jesus.
   By losing one's life, one saves it.

Of all the books of the Bible, Deuteronomy reflects
most often on obedience. At times, as here, the words
are stern: "if you obey . . ., you will live . . . [but] if,
however, you turn away your hearts and will not listen,
. . . you will certainly perish . . . I set before you life
and death, the blessing and the curse." Yet, even here,
as so frequently throughout the book, Deuteronomy
repeats the call to love the Lord, your God. "Choose
life, then, that you and your descendants may live, by
loving the Lord, your God, heeding his voice, and holding fast to him." In fact, Jesus quoted from Deuteronomy when he declared what was the first and greatest
commandment:

> Hear, O Israel! The Lord is our God,
> the Lord alone! Therefore, you shall
> love the Lord, your God, with all your
> heart, and with all your soul, and
> with all your strength (Deut 6:4-5;
> Luke 10:27).

Wherever love is total, spontaneous, and springing
from the depths of life, its every wish is a command!
Obedience expresses the deepest law of existence in
that person. Disobedience, even in a small matter, can
be disastrous, for it disrupts a basic attitude or essential
disposition. Love normally expresses itself in small,
delicate ways. Not to obey such impulses is to tear out
the roots of one's life. "Choose life, then, that you and

your descendants may *live by loving* the Lord, your God, *by heeding his voice*, and *holding fast* to him."

Jesus, nonetheless, tells us in today's gospel not to choose life but to lose it and only thus will we save life! When Deuteronomy admonishes us to "choose life," it does not mean to seek a selfish, narrow, biased existence but rather a life of compassion, concern and help towards one's neighbor. When the laws of Deuteronomy are compared with laws in other books of the Bible, Deuteronomy is marked by exquisite thoughtfulness. It modifies the third commandment about each person's resting on the Sabbath day, even the slaves, by adding the reminder that "you too were once slaves in Egypt" and longed for a day of rest. Perfection and loving obedience brought Jesus to the cross, seeming to lose his life, that a new and greater life resurrect at the end of the way of the cross, Jesus, who loved to quote from Deuteronomy, not only learned much from the book, but also brought its message to a new perfection.

Deuteronomy calls "heaven and earth to witness." Love and obedience summon us out of our tiny, narrow, selfish world into the wide arena of heaven and earth. We are to die to narrow concerns and prejudice, to break down all barriers to justice and neighborly love. God tells us to obey a summons of total love. We must lose the narrow-minded false life, and by its death we rise to true life. If we do not lose this tiny life, then its narrow confines will themselves close in upon us and destroy us.

> Happy are they who hope in the Lord.
> They are like a tree
>   planted near running water,
> That yields its fruit in due season,
>   and whose leaves never fade.

Friday after Ash Wednesday

Is 58:1-9. Fasting should so unite us that everyone realizes how much they depend upon the other and all depend at once upon God. Together we remove one another's yoke.

Matt 9:14-16. Jesus' disciples shall fast when he, the bridegroom, is taken away from them.

Each of us is tempted like the people in Isaiah's prophecy; we feel like saying to God: "Why do we fast, and you do not see it? Afflict ourselves, and you take no note of it?" These temptations invade our mind and unsettle us, even though the answer to the question is so obvious. We do not fast to get something out of it! We do not pray so as to have bargaining power with God. We do not "use" religion, for that would mean manipulating God, any more than we should use people, much less our friends and loved ones.

If we fast to get something out of it from God, we are like poverty-stricken persons who use their poverty to play upon other people's emotions. No matter how destitute, no one is justified, using their children to get donations, displaying them naked and hungry to solicit help. Such a parent almost forces the children to be hungry and naked in order to make a better living for themselves. The prophet Hosea in condemning such people included religious leaders: "they feed on the sin of my people and are greedy for their guilt" (Hos 4:8). These persons become addicts at being poor and keeping their family poor. Neither is it right for us to fast in order to be seen, and thus to move God to pity.

We fast in order to unite ourselves with the poor— to taste their empty lives, to weep over their sad and hungry children, to feel their helplessness. By fasting and giving alms, by sharing our bread and sheltering the oppressed, we stop *turning our back on our own*, as Isaiah announced. Fasting then reunites us with our true family. We the orphan find our way home. Fasting is the way towards home. Home is God's family of the entire human race where the majority go to bed hungry.

Along this way the poor, the hungry and the oppressed lift a yoke from our back. We have been weighed down by a yoke of pride, self-assurance, security and excessive needs. We have been hounded by diets and wasted food and yet we are never satisfied. We carry the yoke of always wanting more and needing more, so that even on our fast days we fall into the trap of carrying out our own pursuits and of quarreling with one another.

Fasting, by uniting us in the family of the poor, teaches us the true values of home life. To be united with the poor is far superior to the most advanced education and certainly to the most elegant entertainment. Through fasting the poor lift these yokes of false values off our shoulders, as by means of the same fasting we share bread with the hungry, shelter the oppressed and homeless, clothe the naked and stop turning our back on our own flesh.

As the poor share with us their sorrow and their mourning over the absence of Jesus, Creator and Provider, the poor lead us home, mysteriously enough to Jesus. In the desire of Jesus, a new love is born, and love always unites and begets new life. The poor lead us then to the marriage feast of the lamb (Rev 19:6-8). No longer, as Jesus says, can the wedding guests go in mourning; the groom is with them.

A broken, humbled heart, O Lord,
     you will not scorn.
Have mercy on me, O God, in your goodness.

Saturday After Ash Wednesday

Is 58:9-14. "If you remove . . . oppression . . . and . . .
    bestow your bread on the hungry . . . then light shall
    rise for you in the darkness . . . the Lord will renew
    your strength."

Luke 5:27-32. Jesus eats and drinks "with tax collectors
    and non-observers of the law." He has come to call
    sinners to a change of heart.

Towards the end of Chapter 58 Isaiah reflects on
the honor and delight of the sabbath law. Jesus disre-
gards aspects of that law by eating and drinking with
people considered contaminated and unclean. In breaking the law, Jesus was very obedient to the principal
purpose of the law, the liberation of God's people from
oppression and the union of this, His chosen people, in
a common bond of blood and compassion (see Lev 25).
God had not summoned Abraham, Moses, David or any
religious leader to save those already saved. As God
had already announced to Moses in summoning him to
lead his people out of Egypt: "I have witnessed the
affliction of my people. . . . I know well what they are
suffering. Therefore I have come down to rescue them"
(Ex 3:7-8).

The compassion of Jesus for sinners, for the poor
and persecuted and for those outside the law, was already anticipated by Isaiah: "If only you remove from
your midst oppression, false accusation and malicious
speech . . ." We need the example of Jesus to put flesh
and sinew around Isaiah's words, before we take the
prophet seriously or even hear what he says. Yet Jesus
himself was criticized for being non-observant and for
disregarding God's laws. Today, Jesus may come to us,
as to the chosen people in his own day, among the
secular, non-observant, unchurched people of the

world. Their warmth, compassion, dedication to the
poor and oppressed, may teach us an important lesson.

In the very best tradition, the law frees us from
"seeking your own interests or speaking with malice."
The Sabbath law in particular enables us to "delight in
the Lord." The Sabbath allows all of us, no matter what
may be our wealth or lack of it, social status or education, to be all equal, all one family, before the law. This
law then frees us from being oppressed by pride, divi-
sion and suspicion.

Both biblical readings for this day allude to the
heavenly banquet. Isaiah sees the ancient ruins rebuilt
and in our new homes we delight in the Lord as he
nourishes us with the good produce of the Promised
Land. Jesus' eating and drinking at the great reception
given in his honor by Levi anticipates heaven when all
sinners — namely, all of us men and women — will have
been invited home to rejoice together as one family. The
Eucharistic service this day participates in their
heavenly banquet.

> You, O Lord, are good and forgiving
>   abounding in kindness to all who call
>   upon you.
> Hearken, O Lord, to my prayer.

FIRST WEEK OF LENT

Monday — First Week of Lent

Lev 19:1-2, 11-18. The Old Testament commentary on the Ten Commandments, concluding with the injunction to "love your neighbor as yourself."

Matt 25:31-46. Final judgment scene, in which eternity is a continuation and ratification of our attitude towards our neighbor on earth.

Both biblical readings deal, like the prophets, with the radical needs and essential elements of human existence. There is no quibbling over small details and luxury items. It becomes a case of life and death, of hunger and thirst, of nakedness and imprisonment. The Scriptures examine our conscience on authentic, basic issues: a blind person, in danger of walking into a stumbling block; a deaf person, abused helplessly with offensive language; a day laborer, prevented from taking home a proper wage to the weakened bodies and dismal eyes of the family.

When issues reach this deeply into the human heart and penetrate so thoroughly into the fibre of human existence, then we come to grips with the most important qualities of life and character. At moments such as these, it is a matter of heaven or hell, life or death, that we put away all grudges and hatred from our hearts, that we forget about revenge and petty quarreling. As Leviticus then concludes: "You shall love your neighbor as yourself."

Lenten fast and penance, Lenten almsgiving and support, Lenten prayer and Bible study — practises such as these unite all men and women. The wealthier taste the hunger of those more poor than themselves, those more poor share their own heroic dependence on

God and their neighbor with the wealthier who can otherwise become too independent and self-sufficient. By these alms the proud can offer the destitute an opportunity for self-respect; by their gracious acceptance the poor can teach the proud how to be of humble heart before God and neighbor.

The book of Leviticus then shouts the deepest laws of creation where we are reduced to that wonderful, common status, all children of God. Therefore, "love your neighbor as yourself." Unless this divine law is pursued and obediently followed, then at the end of life Jesus can do nothing else but say: "I do not know you!" The final judgment is a solemn ratification of how we have responded to the basic laws of human nature— and here we find the wonderful vision of Jesus: "As often as you did it for one of my least brothers and sisters, you did it for me." Jesus too is bone of our bones, flesh of our flesh.

> The law of the Lord is perfect,
>   refreshing the soul;
> The decree of the Lord is trustworthy,
>   giving wisdom to the simple.

Tuesday—First Week of Lent

Isaiah 55:10-11. God's word soaks into our human situation like gentle rain upon the earth, and effectively returns to God in our words and actions.

Matt 6:5-17. Matthew's rendition of the Our Father and the necessity to forgive one another.

Year after year, one Lent after another, we hear and ponder God's word. The process is a long one, of listening to the word of God, of appreciating and absorbing it, of responding to it obediently, so that the word begins to take possession of us, transforms our thoughts and values, and allows our mind and heart to resonate the thoughts and loves of God Himself. This cycle of life is symbolized by rain and snow, falling gently from the sky and soaking the earth with nourishment, then returning towards heaven as bushes and trees. Divine inspiration is the rain and snow, our inspired lives are the bushes and trees. This image concludes chapters forty to fifty-five of Isaiah, some of the most enthusiastic and tragic literature of the Old Testament.

The lines of this exalted poetry show all the hallmarks of human genius, well trained and carefully exercised. The poems, moreover, seethe with hopes and ideals, with courage and persistency, superceding normal human power. As we today contemplate chapters forty to fifty-five, we sense the divine word reaching through our human words back to God in superhuman ways.

We do not know the name of the author of this sublime poetry; sometimes the author is called "Second Isaiah" or even the "Great Unknown." So thoroughly did his message clothe his personality, that his name is lost; the word becomes translucently God's word! Yet, the lines redound with tender and exquisite human compassion; they pulse with the flesh and blood, the breath and heart of our life.

"See!" God says through this prophet, "upon the palms of my hands I have written your name" (Is 49:16). Again we read God's explanation: "because you are precious in my eyes and glorious, and because I love you" (43:4).

In order that this tender growth reach towards God over a long period of time, God's interior life within ourselves and within others must be delicately nourished and gently loved. Such love is best expressed by bestowing great hopes and unconditional forgiveness. And this is exactly the type of love which Jesus teaches us when he taught us to pray the *Our Father*. Hope, confidence and security are planted in our hearts and genuinely confessed, when we say:

> Your kingdom come.
> Your will be done on earth as it is in heaven.
> Give us today our daily bread,
> forgive us
> and deliver us

These beautiful words—of bursting sunrise, of kingdom come, of sweet smelling fresh bread, of gentle forgiveness from depths of understanding, of deliverance from all anxiety, of soothing every wrong—allow a delicate new life with warmth, hope and love to develop, from a new embryo into a fully formed man and woman of God.

A gentle, persistent concern reaches us through the penance and prayer of Lent. This year is not just another Lent, but a fuller divine word, within us, "achieving the end for which I sent it."

> From all their afflictions
>   God will deliver the just.
> Look to him that you may be radiant with joy.

Wednesday—First Week of Lent
Jonah 3:1-10. At the preaching of Jonah, the inhabitants of the Assyrian capital of Nineveh, all pagans, from

king and nobles to every human person, and even the
animals, fast from food and drink; the people repent
and pray for mercy.

Luke 11:29-32. Jesus' preaching, life and very person
were "greater than Jonah," his "wisdom . . . greater
than Solomon," yet Jesus was not accepted.

The inspired author of the book of *Jonah* knew his
Bible and his sacred history extremely well. He weaves
into his narrative phrases, ideas and allusions from
many other parts of the Sacred Scripture or from Israel's sacred tradition. The words of the Assyrian king,
"Who knows God may relent and forgive, and withhold
his blazing wrath," are drawn from earlier biblical texts
like the penitential prayer in Joel 2:14. The inspired
author, then, had meditated so long on his Bible, that
his own preaching and writing became a filigree or
tapestry of passages from the Bible.

Because he knew his religion so very well, that he
could think and dream only in its language, the author of
Jonah almost exploded with exasperation and frustration. Why do those people—his own—with such a rich
heritage, refuse to reform their ways and respond to
God with faith and justice, with prayer and hope? Look,
says this writer, the pagans, even the worst of them, the
ruthless and ever hated Assyrians, are more spontaneously good than my own people!

The book of *Jonah* prepares us for the most wonderful of surprises, the extraordinary and unsuspected
goodness of strangers, even of such unlikely candidates
for holiness as . . . . The dotted lines must be filled in by
each one of us; here we name our worst enemy, our
most impossible sinner, hopelessly wicked to the mar-
row of the bones. Such is the "Assyrian". People today

use such words as Huns or Communist or Nazi!

The message of today's Bible readings can be summed up in that one word, *hope*! We must never lose hope in others and in ourselves, in world affairs, in the national political scene. So surely—at the preaching of Jonah, and we have someone far greater than Jonah— conversions and transformations can take place. Not just an isolated individual, but families, neighborhoods and countries—the entire city of Nineveh—can believe in God, proclaim a fast, pray for forgiveness, and become a model of goodness for all the rest of us pseudo-saints! Hope can and will come from the least suspected quarters, whether in secret corners of our own hearts or of others.

Jonah announces the tremendous depths of hidden goodness in all of us and in our entire world.

Jonah instructs us in the power and necessity of decisions. The king of Nineveh *at once* "rose from his throne . . . and sat in the ashes."

Jonah offers us a glimpse, baffling and enticing, into the heart of God. The Bible states that when God saw the *repentance* of Nineveh, then he himself "*repented* of the *evil* he had threatened to do to them; he did not carry it out." If God then can humbly change his mind, how can we remain rigidly self-righteous and condemnatory of others!

At the preaching of Jonah they reformed, but you have a greater than Jonah here.

> A clean heart create for me, O God,
>> And a steadfast spirit renew within me,
> A broken, humbled heart
>> O God, you will not scorn.

Thursday—First Week of Lent

Esther 12:14-16, 23-25. Esther reminds God of his past
favors towards Israel, his own people chosen from all
others, and begs for his assistance now in her loneliness and helplessness.

Matt 7:7-12. Ask and you shall receive . . . how much
more will your heavenly Father give good things.

The book of Esther exemplifies and so establishes
the promise of Jesus: ask and you shall receive. God
heard her prayer and acted to save his chosen people
Israel.

It is true that from a moral viewpoint Esther had no
choice but to present herself before the Persian king.
Such a bold and abrupt act could cost her life. Yet to do
nothing would mean sitting idly and safely in an ivory
tower while all her own people were destroyed—and
live haunted with the guilt that she might have saved her
people or else would have shared in the honor of their
martyrdom. Life, at least at times, is worth living only
in the heights of heroic action. There are occasions in
the existence of each person when heroic action is
obligatory.

These moments usually turn out to be very lonely
stretches of our existence. Perhaps, no one else will
understand, but in any case we alone must make the
decision which decides between martyrdom or
perpetual guilt. Esther prays: "My Lord, our king, you
alone are God. Help me, who am alone and have no help
but you."

Times such as these lead to experiences of mystic
prayer. Fantasies of ambition, pretensions of strength,
selfish motivations, reliance upon wit and diplomacy
and half-truths—all of these weakening and con-

taminating elements are swept out of our memory. Every crutch is taken away, and if we are to stand, it is through God's strength alone. If we are to look, it is like staring into the sun. We see a vision of God, so overwhelming that all is darkness. Our feelings seem cold and unresponsive, yet we sense an extraordinary excitement at the base of our existence, stirred by God's mysterious love for us.

Prayer at such times is bound to be heard, just because we are in touch with the best and most beautiful part of ourselves, with the depths that support all else about ourselves, with the Creator whose loving plan called us into life and who alone knows the whole secret of our future.

Such prayers again will be answered, far beyond our best hopes, because we place no conditions on what God can accomplish within us. "Would one of you hand their child a stone if the child asks for bread? . . . If you, with all your sins, know how to give your children what is good, how much more will your heavenly Father give good things to anyone who asks him?" Prayer when we do not know the outcome, is always a scary matter. God may even respond with a miracle—a miracle which cuts through the human process to fulfill the humanly impossible, or a miracle of grace to suffer and die with martyrdom!

This prayer is not irrational, even though it reaches far beyond the rational possibilities of human life. It is founded upon the memory of God's great redemptive acts for Israel. Esther prayed: "You, O Lord, chose . . . our ancestors . . . and fulfilled all your promises to them. . . . Be mindful of us, O Lord. Manifest yourself in the time of our distress . . . Help me, who am alone and have no one but you, O Lord."

"Ask and you shall receive . . . how much more will your heavenly Father give good things."

Lord, on this day, I called for help,
　　　　　You answered me.

Friday — First Week of Lent

Ez 18:21-28. If wicked persons turn away from all their sins, they shall surely live, they shall not die.

Matt 5:20-26. Anyone who grows angry with his brother or sister shall be liable to the judgment.

The prophet Ezekiel places before us God's expectation that we persevere in doing good across a lifetime. In Matthew's gospel Jesus roots this expectation in the depths of the heart. We must do more than externally avoid murdering our brother or sister; we must interiorly be at peace with them and never harbor anger or resentment.

Jesus also *names* the recipient of our patience and kindliness; he calls this person our brother or our sister. At first, this designation might seem to make the practice of tolerance and helpfulness all the easier. Yet our common experience tells us that we lose our temper more quickly and muster the strength to forgive far more slowly in the case of our own family, relation or neighborhood. Family feuds flare up unexpectedly and last for generations.

Once we are reconciled in our hearts, as Jesus expects, then the prophet Ezekiel declares that this new relationship of trust, compassion and assistance must not be a quick, momentary expression. It is not to be easily forgotten as we conveniently avoid our newly found brother or sister for the rest of our life. Consistently and daily we are expected to live together as one family.

This continuous bond of affection and mutual help is so important that Jesus states: "If you bring your gift to the altar and then recall that your brother or sister has anything against you, go first to be reconciled with your brother or sister, and then come and offer your gift." These words sear a quick, straight path into our conscience, as we are gathered around our Eucharistic table.

This journey to our brother or sister can be made in our heart first; we form a *determination* to do all in our power to win back our brother or sister. On that condition which practically asks us to be forgiving, patient, and tolerant of differences, we can continue with our Eucharist. If we fail, however, to carry through on our promise and ignore our brother or sister, then Ezekiel rings out the deadly warning: "If the virtuous person turns from the path of virtue to do evil . . . has broken faith and committed sin, . . . he shall die!"

These divine expectations, enunciated by Ezekiel and Jesus, touch at times upon the heroic, as we are not asked but commanded to forgive and be reconciled, on pain of death and the fires of Gehenna. Does God ask too much? God asks nothing without first giving us the grace of a "new heart and . . . a new spirit" and putting his own spirit within us (see Ez 36:26-27). Secondly, God provides his own compelling example. In Ezekiel God assures us that no matter how wickedly we have offended him—whatever be the offense against life and goodness—God forgives *at once* if we turn from our evil ways. Ezekiel concludes this extraordinary chapter with God's admission, "I have no pleasure in the death of anyone who dies . . . Return and live!"

> Out of the depths I cry to you, O Lord;
> Lord, hear my voice.

Saturday—First Week of Lent

Deut 26:16-19. God wants his laws observed "with all your heart and . . . soul" as "today you are to be a people peculiarly his own."

Matt 5:43-48. "Love your enemies. . . . You must be made perfect as your heavenly Father is perfect."

God first chose Israel, and within Israel He included each of us as "a people peculiarly his own." God first took the initiative to make his presence known within the depths of our mind and heart where we reach out to form family, within the subconscious of our memory which reaches into the lives of our parents and ancestors, within the customs of our faith where we echo the prayer and the traditions of our church. Jesus adds that God's call surrounds us like the sun and rain. While we are still asleep, God summons his creature the sun to rise and spread a burst of light across our day; while we are distracted by duties and grumbling about the drought, God orders the rain to drop moisture upon our dry earth and weary hearts. God *first* loves us.

Just as God acts out of love, he wants each of us to respond accordingly "with all your heart and with all your soul." God is not simply a distant giant in charge of a mammoth computer machine; the sun does not rise nor the rain fall simply by God's light touch upon the keys of the computer. Rather, God sees our need for light and warmth, for rain water and cool moisture, and each day out of love he makes the proper decision, continuing to care even for those who hate him and disregard him. God first loves us from the depth of his mind and heart.

Because God's loving concern is renewed each day—yet continues with persevering strength—the book of Deuteronomy returns repeatedly to one of its favorite themes: *today*. In the reading of Chapter 26, as earlier in Chapter 5, we are advised: "*today* you are making this agreement with the Lord." God's deeply embedded love, thoroughly within the heart and soul, within the fibers of bone and muscle, must not become lost in the shadows or abysses of our existence. As with God so with us, it needs to be renewed *each day*. In fact, Chapter 1 of Joshua picks up phrases from this passage of Deuteronomy, and extends the *today* of Deuteronomy into a recital of God's love and our loving response "by day and by night" (Josh 1:8).

Day by day, hour by hour we ought to be re-dedicating ourselves to God, in good circumstances and bad ones, with friends and with enemies, in sunlight and in dark rainy stretches. The beat of our heart ought to be responding to God's beat, the intake of our life-breath to the breathing of God's spirit upon us. God first loves us with heart and soul moment by moment, and to *live* we must resonate or vibrate this divine heartbeat and breathing of life. And so we will "be made perfect as your heavenly Father is perfect."

To absorb this divine perfection is not just an heroic effort on our part—we must summon all our energy of mind and heart to this enterprise—but it is mostly the result of beating with God's heart and breathing with his spirit, of reacting to God's initiative, therefore of surrendering to God with all our heart and mind.

Lent, therefore, is a time of fasting and prayer, of much human work and dedication, but only that we may be so disposed that the beat of God's heart and the rhythm of his spirit take possession of ours.

> Happy are they who follow the law of the
> Lord.
> I will give you thanks with an upright heart,
> when I have learned your just
> ordinances.

SECOND WEEK OF LENT

Monday—Second Week of Lent

Dan 9:4-10. "With fasting, sackcloth, and ashes," Daniel confesses shamefacedly the sins of the people of Israel and appeals to God's "compassion and forgiveness."

Luke 6:36-38. "Be compassionate, as your Father is compassionate. Do not judge, and you will not be judged."

Where Matthew's gospel quotes Jesus as saying: "You must be made perfect as your heavenly Father is perfect" (Matt 5:48), Luke reads: "Be compassionate, as your Father is compassionate." Luke's expectations are more specific and more attainable. All sinners ought to be capable of compassion, as they continually seek this very response of mercy from God. Yet, Jesus does not allow half-measures; it must be all, it seems, or nothing! Pardon must be bestowed so generously upon anyone who has hurt us, that it runs over and pours into the folds of one's own garments. We are expected to bestow twice as much love as the other person showed us hate, twice as much trust as the other party manifested suspicion.

This divine compassion can be partly learned, as we meditate upon the example of Jesus who died for us when as yet we were God's enemies by our sins (Rom 5:8). Yet, this attitude of overwhelming goodness and understanding can never be fully and adequately learned by study nor be acquired by human effort, no matter how diligent and persevering we may be. We cannot transform ourselves into God, as the human race should have learned at the beginning (Gen 3:5).

23

The only way to surrender ourselves to God is unconditionally and without reservation. Without anticipating all that will happen to us and be asked of us, we give ourselves totally into God's hands. We repeat Jesus' beautiful, heroic prayer: "not my will but yours be done" (Luke 22:42). God will then act through us, reaching others with infinite compassion, infinite tenderness, infinite trust! Without counting the cost or the outcome, such divine life will overflow into the folds of our garments!

Lenten fasting may weaken our physical strength and reduce the aggressiveness of our human response. If it is accompanied, however, by a surrender of our spirit to God, then divine strength and infinite responsiveness will flow through us. Our fasting reminds us and symbolizes to others that God alone is the source of our decisions and actions.

Possessed by this divine spirit of compassion and pardon, we can spontaneously pray for mercy as Daniel did in today's first reading. We have only to place before God our sins, our wickedness and our evil. We have only to admit to God that "we have rebelled and departed from your commandments and laws." We realize that in confessing our sins, we are already within the intimate bond of God's love and transformation. Confession is the final act of rejecting whatever is the residue of sin within us. Once upon our lips, the sins are gone forever, driven out by God's holy spirit already within us.

Daniel admits several times to be "shamefaced." Shame can be very destructive or it can be purifying and transforming. Sometimes when shame comes over people, they lose all inhibitions and abandon themselves to all kinds of shameless deeds! Another kind of shame casts off pride and make-belief. It begets a wholesome humility and honesty. It freely admits whatever was wrong, this time from the attitude of a delicate conscience. It helps the adult to be again as a child in spirit, in trust, in a wholesome purity. Such an adult trusts, loves and forgives as easily as God himself. "Of such is the kingdom of God."

> Lord, do not deal with us as our sins deserve.
>> may your compassion quickly come to us,
>> for we are brought very low.

Tuesday—Second Week of Lent

Is 1:10, 16-20. Make justice your aim by caring for the needy, then your sins will be removed.

Matt 23:1-12. Do not seek to appear holy nor to be given honorary titles. Humble yourselves.

The Scriptures for this day inculcate consistency and integral wholeness of life. All must fit together: thoughts and actions, interior esteem and exterior forms of justice. This harmonious interaction reaches outward, beyond one's clothing and titles, beyond one's immediate circle of friends and acquaintances, to all the poor and needy within reach and beyond! "Redress the wronged, hear the orphan's plea and defend the widow."

Orphan and widow symbolize in the Bible *all* the helpless and indigent people of the world. Isaiah the prophet mentions them after a stern and fearsome passage, omitted in the liturgy. To neglect the poor while spreading out one's hands in prayer to God forces from

God the terrifying response: "I close my eyes to you
. . . I will not listen." In fact, such indifference towards
the poor, God declares, makes "your hands . . . full of
blood!" The prophet must have shouted the next
phrase. "Wash yourselves clean!" How?—by attend-
ing to the orphan and widow.

The poor, consequently, are members of one's own
family, one's own wife and children, those left behind
without protection. The entire family must close ranks
around its own flesh and blood. Not to do so makes it
guilty of blood!

We all shudder, for we have all passed by a beggar
without giving alms. We have all driven comfortably
through slums. We have wasted food in the same city
where widow and orphan were going to bed with aching
hearts and pinched stomachs. We are frightened as God
shouts in his indignation: "Come now, let us set things
right!"

Despite such serious sins—sins of omission to feed
the starving and to defend the helpless—God offers the
possibility of total conversion. "Though your sins be
like scarlet, they may become white as snow; though
they be crimson red, they may become white as wool."

God, too, is totally consistent, just as he demands
of us. God does not leave us sinful at heart and simply
clothe us with a beautiful appearance—with the
phylacteries and tassels of holiness! We are totally
transformed. He alone is our teacher, our father, our
messiah, our all. Therefore, we are guided by God,
enlivened by God, saved by God—totally God's
through and through.

Our initial fear suddenly changes into the peace,
joy and security of the blessed. We find that the
heavenly family closes ranks around us because we

have gathered the poor within our earthly family. Because we have served the lowly, we are gathered into the assembly of the great saints; because we have humbled ourselves to be one family with the oppressed, we are exalted to the company of God's favorites.

All this happens "if you are willing and obey." "But if you refuse and resist, the sword shall consume you, for the mouth of the Lord has spoken." We may question if Isaiah's consoling message of forgiveness and new life should end on such a terrifying note. Consistency and integral wholeness are a matter of life or death, of family or disintegration. The offer of total love has no other option.

To the upright
I will show the saving power of God.

Wednesday — Second Week of Lent

Jer 18:18-20. In this fourth "confession" of Jeremiah, the prophet complains to God about the people conspiring against him.

Matt 20:17-28. To aspire to greatness, we must serve the needs of all, even to the point of offering our lives for them.

Both biblical readings record an intrigue to get ahead! Jeremiah's own family had already turned against him (Jer 12:6-23), and now the religious and secular authorities contrive a plot to do away with this troublesome challenger. In Matthew's gospel "the mother of Zebedee's sons," James and John (see Matt 4:21), seeks to maneuver a secret promise from Jesus "that these sons of mine will sit, one at your right hand

and the other at your left, in your kingdom." God's plans are not to be advanced in the way of personal ambition or double-dealing!

Jeremiah states the *initial*, essential attitude for all religious work: *prayer for the welfare of others*. "Heed me, O Lord! . . . Remember that I stood before you to speak in their behalf, to turn away your wrath from them." We seek *their* goodness, *their* peace, *their* life. These gifts come from the Lord and must be sought from him. Jeremiah's apostolic activity redounded from the remembrance of the Lord and His plans and hopes for others.

The concluding verses of Jeremiah's "confession" seem to reverse this attitude and demand revenge and pain from God upon these same people, now the prophet's persecutors. It is important to recall, however, that these five "confessions" of Jeremiah (12:1-5; 15:10-11, 15-21; 17:14-18; 18:19-23; and 20:7-18) originally formed a separate scroll (or booklet) composed in the form of a personal diary and were never intended for public eyes. The editor of the book of Jeremiah found this diary, after completing the initial draft of his manuscript—in fact, after the prophet's death—and inserted these profoundly personal documents where he felt they belonged historically. When Jeremiah curses his enemies, he is not necessarily proud of himself. He is simply honest and open before God, saying, as it were: "Here, God, is how I feel. Help!"

If Jeremiah turned to God in prayer for others and for himself, then he firmly believed in God's mysterious plan for all his people. Here then is the *second*, essential attitude for apostolic undertaking: to seek the Lord's will. We must believe that such a plan exists *in God*. The *Epistle to the Ephesians* calls it "God's secret plan'' (Eph 3:3, 9), ''the mysterious design which for ages was hidden in God, the Creator of all''. Before his resurrection, Jesus did not know this plan thoroughly (Matt 24:36) and so he was unable to promise personal privileges to James and John. We too must not seek special status nor labor for our own benefit nor seek to fulfill ambitions. Only by being absorbed in prayer can we begin to sense intuitively a small part of ''God's secret plan.'' Such prayer keeps our activity closer in touch with God's hopes.

Personal disinterestedness is clearly enunciated by Jesus. The gospel selection begins and ends with an announcement of Jesus' death. He ''has come, not to be served by others, but to serve, to give his own life.'' Conversions and other apostolic achievements are godly only when they serve to humiliate the apostle before the goodness of others and before the wonder of God.

> My trust is in you, O Lord;
>> I say, "You are my God."
> In your hands is my destiny; rescue me.

Thursday—Second Week of Lent

Jer 17:5-10. Cursed be the one who trusts in humankind alone.

Lk 16:19-31. Parable of the rich person Dives and the poor man Lazarus.

Lent is not only a time for prolonged and more frequent prayer, but this holy season enables us to purify our motives for prayer. Prayer is not a bargaining time, to trade our pious words for God's gifts.

In the pronouncement of Jeremiah and the parable of Jesus we meet a lifetime of seeming barrenness, of apparent salty waste, of unrelieved poverty. Even "the person who trusts in the Lord" faces the fierce heat of the desert wilderness and "the year of drought." On the surface of it life is surrounded by the same burnt out dryness for the good person and for the other "one who trusts [only] in human beings . . . whose heart turns away from the Lord."

In Jesus' parable the imagery changes from the desert wilderness in Jeremiah's statement to the gate of a wealthy person's villa. Inside is daily feasting, outside destitution. After Dives would wipe his mouth and hands with a piece of bread, he would toss the bread away. Lazarus considered himself lucky to snatch these crumbs to stay alive. Lazarus managed barely to survive in his own kind of salty waste!

Jeremiah's poem compares the two persons still further. "The one who trusts [only] in human beings, who seeks his strength in flesh, whose heart is turned away from the Lord . . . is like a barren bush" without fruit, fit only for kindling wood. The other bush, typified by "the person who trusts in the Lord, whose hope is the Lord," is surrounded with the same dry sand, yet continues to bear fruit. The roots sink deeply beneath the surface into the hidden water of God's holy will.

This description fits Jeremiah himself. His life seemed to be in shambles, even his own family turned against him (Jer 11:19-23; 12:6); the king Zedekiah befriended him only in secret and left him to his enemies in daylight (Jer 37). The prophet died, persecuted, in the foreign land of Egypt (Jer 43). Yet, with his roots searching deeply for God's will, Jeremiah became one of the most crucial figures in the history of Israel's religion. His influence upon the popular devotion of the people turned out to be as profound as anyone else's in Israel's long history. The book of Jeremiah sustained Jesus in prayer and continues to be our source of strength. While Jeremiah considered himself useless (15:10-21), he was supporting a nation.

Jeremiah was bearing fruit, and Lazarus too must have evinced an exceptional dignity and wholesomeness even though sitting with dogs and begging for crumbs at Dives' parlor door! Destitution in some cases can destroy the last shreds of self-respect, but in other cases it can and does force the *inner* peace and strength of a person to appear translucent across the face and in the entire bearing of the beggar. There are no jewels and other cosmetics to hide or distract from the spiritual goodness at the heart.

Only this interior goodness survives into eternity, as only this sinking of one's tap root in God's holy will allows a person to absorb interior nourishment. External changes of temperature, rain or sunshine, floods or droughts, do not destroy such life, for it does not depend upon the surface events. Even if there were visions and revelations, even if the holiest of people like Lazarus returned from Paradise to planet earth, still such extraordinary episodes will not bring the recipient across the desert stretch of dryness nor induce him to give up his sham of luxury and his callousness to injustice.

We pray, therefore, not for short term gifts, nor for feelings and manifestations of holiness. True, we can ask God's help in such matters, but basically we pray that the hopes and the beat of our heart, the sight of our eyes, the strength of our bearing manifest that "blessed . . . person who trusts [always] in the Lord."

> Happy are they who hope in the Lord.
> They are like a tree
> > planted near running water,
> That yields its fruit in due season,
> > And whose leaves never fade.

Friday—Second Week of Lent
Gen 37:3-4, 12-13a, 17b-28. Joseph is sold into slavery by his jealous brothers.
Matt 21:33-43, 45-46. Parable of the unjust and rapacious servants who eventually kill the owner's son. The vineyard will be given to others who will yield a rich harvest.

Beginning with Chapter 37 the story of Joseph occupies a major section in the first book of the Bible (Gen 37-50) and, in fact, concludes the book of Genesis. The account of Joseph has one overriding motif which is stated at the end in Joseph's words to his brothers: "Have no fear. Can I take the place of God? Even though you meant harm to me, God meant it for good, to achieve his present end, the survival of many people" (50:19-20).

Mysteriously yet powerfully God brings our convoluted, mixed-up and even betrayed life to an overflow of goodness, even for our enemies and for those who cared little for us. In Joseph's case the twelve tribes are securely established in Egypt where they multiply and develop a distinctive culture and strong unity. In Jesus' case his rejection by the Jewish leaders would lead to a new and more glorious Israel, joining Jew and Gentile in one family (Romans, ch 11).

The story of Joseph and the ministry of Jesus exemplify our faith in God's providence. A divine plan reaches into the depth of our existence. At times we may reach a clear though passing glimpse of it, other times we intuit it during long periods of prayer, yet always we are being directed and guided by it. Jesus refers to this overwhelming plan of his Heavenly Father in his frequent references to the Hebrew scriptures. There must exist a large, world plan in the mind of God, culminating in Jesus. In fact during this parable Jesus quotes from Psalm 118:

The stone which the builders rejected
has become the keystone of the structure.
It was the Lord who did this
and we find it marvelous to behold
(Ps 118:22-23)

In the story of Joseph this same faith in God's providential care is proposed in the references to dreams. In fact, the other brothers nickname Joseph "the master dreamer." Not only in Chapter 37 but later in an Egyptian prison Joseph gains his freedom and eventually a high position at the royal court by interpreting dreams (Gen 40-41). In the Bible dreams symbolize the hidden, mysterious, deeply imbedded and sure way by which God's providential plan comes to human consciousness. Through these dreams Joseph confesses a profound belief in God's continuous love and guidance.

Lenten fasts and prayers ought to purify our minds

and hearts and so put us into closer touch with the
depths of ourselves where God resides. Selfishness and
false ambition, sensuality and over-confidence should
be swept away by our sacrifices, Bible study and other
devotional practices. We should begin all over again to
"dream" our best yet hidden ideals, planted in us by
God. We should feel a renewal of peace and strength, a
conviction that God's mysterious yet most real providence is taking even more effective control of our lives.
More and more we should acquire serenity even in the
face of problems, disappointments and perhaps betrayal. "God meant it for good." These words of Joseph
become our own and we see a marvelous effect, "a rich
harvest."

> Remember the marvels the Lord has done.
> When the Lord called down a famine on the
> > land
> > > and ruined the crop that sustained
> > > them,
> He sent a man before them,
> > Joseph, sold as a slave.

Saturday—Second Week of Lent

Micah 7:14-15, 18-20. An appeal to God for pardon and
compassion towards the flock of his inheritance.
Luke 15:1-3, 11-32. The parable of the prodigal son and
the forgiving father.

In these passages the Bible speaks of an inheritance, promised on earth "to our fathers from days of
old," yet "squandered . . . on dissolute living." In each
case the inheritance has been lost, and yet an underly-

ing continuous trust in God convinces Israel and the prodigal son that the heavenly Father will return what was lost.

The Micah passage concludes the book of this prophet, known for his championing of social justice and the rights of the dispossessed and underprivileged (see ch 2). It seems that the verses (7:11-20) were a later addition, from some anonymous, inspired source, editing this book of the prophet in the post-exilic age.

The people of Judah have seen "her downfall . . . trampled underfoot," as predicted in 7:10; she has been driven off to a foreign land. This disaster was due to the people's sins, insisted the prophet, and must not be explained simplistically by Assyria's and later Babylon's vastly superior army. Even now that the exile has ended and the poverty-stricken people have returned to Jerusalem, they are insignificant—numerically, diplomatically and economically.

The inspired author of these lines begs God to "show us wonderful signs . . . as you have sworn to our fathers from days of old" (v 15, 20). This inheritor of Micah's prophetic mantle weaves earlier biblical passages into his words; we hear echoes of Jer 10:6; Ps 105:6; Is 41:8; 63:16. Pondering these biblical passages not only enabled this person to survive through some dreary, monotonous, small times, but also to continue dreaming of wonderful things. Memory has become the pledge and the hope of the future. It provides the substance of faith and contact with a living compassionate God.

The prodigal son, too, survived on his memories and so was humbly courageous to seek out his father, prodigal with forgiveness. "Coming to his senses at last" meant that the goodness of the father, planted within the bones and blood of the son, finally caught up with the young man and overcame the wayward's resistance. A beautiful touch in Jesus' parable indicates that from a distance the father was beckoning the boy home, before the son ever noticed him. It almost seems as if the father's desire had been reaching across miles and mountains to touch the faith of the son. The son's remembrance might even be like a passive surrender to a hidden stimulant, calling out for love and celebration.

Meditating upon the Holy Scriptures enables us to experience the heavenly Father's presence at the core of our existence. The Bible revives memories and hopes. It brings new life to our best self, planted in us by God. It invigorates the memories about God, inherited from our ancestors—the faithfulness to Jacob, the grace to Abraham. Jacob and Abraham symbolize all the saintly men and women before us. The "wonderful signs" become miracles now!

The most joyful miracle may be our newly found hope. Our greatest gift to future generations will be this remembrance of God's total goodness at the base of our existence. From our heavenly home we can beckon sons and daughters home, as we wait for them. We will enable them to write a new addition to our lives, as lines were once added to Micah's prophecy. They will enable us to celebrate like the father upon the return of the prodigal son. When God's deeply planted life in us makes all these claims come true, the family of God's children will be complete.

> Bless the Lord, O my soul!
>> Forget not all his benefits.
> He pardons all your iniquities,
>> he crowns you with kindness and compassion.

THIRD WEEK OF LENT

Monday—Third Week of Lent

2 Kings 5:1-15a. Naaman, a pagan army commander, is cured of leprosy by the prophet Elisha, by washing seven times in the river Jordan.

Luke 4:24-30. Jesus is rejected by his own home town people at Nazareth for announcing the salvation of foreigners.

At its heart biblical faith includes a belief in miracles. God could and did intervene in human affairs so that dramatic changes and wondrous transformations happened. While miracles took the people by surprise, nonetheless these same people should have been prepared, at least partially, for God's action. By pondering their own sacred traditions, they should have spotted signals of great things to come.

In the days of the prophet Elisha an Israelite slave girl, forced to live among the pagan Arameans, remembered her religious heritage better than the king of Israel. The great acts of God accomplished through Moses, Joshua, Samuel and other religious or civil leaders were reminders of what God could always accomplish. The only condition expected of the people was faith.

Faith put every human resource to work and yet realized at the same time that its hopes and ideals reached beyond these human means and relied upon God. Faith, therefore, was practical and kind enough to muster one's ability and energy for the good of others; it was also humble enough to admit that still more had to be done. A person of faith combined exceptional energy for others, abounding hopes for life, and humble reliance upon God.

Such a person was the Hebrew servant girl in the foreign city of Damascus. Instead of hating her slave master who kept her from her own family, she was concerned about his incurable skin disease. She excelled with hopes for the happiness of others, and she trusted God's power and good judgment.

By contrast, the king of Israel who even enjoyed the benefits of his people's freedom from Egypt and foreign slavery did not believe that God could still liberate the needy and the oppressed. He was so taken up with his own royal status and privileges that he suspected the king of Aram to be "only looking for a quarrel with me!" How limited the hopes and possibilities of a selfish, faithless person. Even in kingly freedom they are more fearful than a slave girl in a foreign household!

Jesus, too, was a slave in a foreign land. This parallel with the Israelite slave girl is drawn from St. Paul's words in the epistle to the Philippians:

> Though he was in the form of God . . .
> he emptied himself
> > and took the form of a slave,
> > being born in human likeness
> > (Phil 2:6-7 CS)

Jesus also remembered his sacred traditions and knew his Bible very well. At Nazareth "he unrolled the scroll [of Isaiah] and found the passage . . .

> The spirit of the Lord is upon me . . .
> > to bring glad tidings to the poor, . . .
> > liberty to captives
> > sight to the blind . . . (Is 61:1)

Jesus would not perform miracles for public esteem or for royal status, neither to heal himself nor to gain prominence "in his native place." Jesus acted out of compassion. Genuine concern reaches through all barriers and acts at once for all races and nationalities, for widows at Zarephath and lepers of Syria. The people at Nazareth should also have known their Bible and have caught the signals. Selfishness, however, filled them with indignation against Jesus and they expelled him.

Faith in miracles lies at the source of the Bible. Such faith requires compassion and hope at the heart of each believer. For God miraculously to reach beyond the laws of nature we must love beyond all restrictions.

> Send forth your light and your fidelity;
> they shall lead me on
> And bring me to your holy mountain,
> to your dwelling place.

Tuesday — Third Week of Lent

Dan 3:25, 34-43. In the aftermath of national disaster Daniel prays for forgiveness and a new chance to follow the Lord unreservedly.

Matt 18:21-35. We must forgive one another, in order to receive forgiveness.

An integral wholeness and thorough consistency dominate these two biblical selections. Even the destruction of Israel's life, as described here in the book of Daniel, is total. "We have in our day no prince, prophet or leader, no holocaust, sacrifice, oblation or incense, no place to offer first fruits, to find favor with you."

These words of lament were uttered from the fiery furnace. All had gone up in flames!

Such totality of destruction is matched by the "whole heart" with which the Lord's servants turn back to him. "We follow you," they declare, "unreservedly." This conversion to the Lord begins with the admission: "we are . . . brought low . . . because of our sins." The inspired writer does not pretend that all is well nor attempt self-justification. He tells it as it is. Earlier in the same chapter he confessed: "We have sinned and transgressed by departing from you, and we have done every kind of evil" (v 29). Total conversion then means an overwhelming experience of God's "kindness and great mercy." God, however, can respond this generously only if his people are honest with themselves. To receive God's forgiveness they must confess their sins.

Nor is this consistent and integral unity to be splintered by a lonely, self-righteous attempt to be saved individually, independent of the community. It seems that the prophet Daniel might have struck out on his own. He could have been saved more quickly and efficiently if he had not been caught within the web of community sin and guilt. However, this chosen people Israel, which was riddled with sin and guilt, was also the source of each individual's hope. The inspired author here appealed to community tradition and their call by God. He prayed to the Lord:

> For your name's sake, do not deliver us up
>> forever,
>> or make void your *covenant*
> Do not take away your mercy from us,
>> for the sake of Abraham, your
>> beloved,
>> Isaac your servant, and Israel your
>> holy one.

From the community he absorbed life with its hopes beyond hope, the divine promises to be "like the stars of heaven."

Another part of the total realism of this prayer appears in the sense of *shame*. In the verse immediately preceding today's liturgical selection the prophet confessed: "We . . . have become a shame and a reproach" (v 33). Such an honest confession of human experience is healthy. There is, nonetheless, another sort of shame which is not good. Again this writer begs of God: "Do not let us be put to shame, but deal with us in your kindness and great mercy." This second kind of shame is harmful for it rejects the remembrance of God's love and has no roots of human dignity.

Just as Daniel and his companions found their lives and their hope integrally within the people of God, the entire community, likewise the parable of Jesus extends this need of consistent wholeness. The forgiveness which is received from God must reach out from us to all our brothers and sisters. "Should you not have dealt mercifully with your fellow servant," the heavenly Father declares, "as I dealt with you?". What we receive from God, makes us to be who we are; we cannot remain who we are unless we give it all away "unreservedly." The gift from God most difficult to share and bestow upon another is forgiveness; yet, this gift is precisely the one of which all of us stand most in need.

By giving we receive, and thus an integral wholeness and thorough consistency of all of us with one another and with God are accomplished. In Lent we seek forgiveness from God. Let us be reconciled with brother and sister.

Good and upright is the Lord;
     thus he shows sinners the way.

He guides the humble to justice,
    he teaches the humble his way.

Wednesday—Third Week of Lent

Deut 4:1, 5-9. Exhortation to obey God's law in view of
    his wisdom and nearness over a long period of time.
Matt 5:17-19. Jesus came to fulfill the law, even in the
    least and smallest part of the letter of the law.

    Deuteronomy reminds us of what is obvious and
yet easily overlooked. In the Bible laws are not obeyed
for their own sake, but rather, they are a way of obeying
God. This fifth book of the Bible is not so much a
"second law" (as the word "Deuteronomy" means in
its Greek origin) but instead a series of fervent homilies
or motivational instructions. Deuteronomy frequently
returns to the idea of "today" as the moment when
Moses receives the law from the Lord and in his name
gives it to all the people. See Deut 5:1-5; 26:16-19. The
people—indeed ourselves—hear God speak "face to
face" (5:4).

    Deuteronomy also describes the attitude for re-
sponding to God, as He speaks to us. "Therefore, *you
shall love the Lord*, your God, with all your heart, and
with all your soul, and with all your strength. Take to
heart these words which I enjoin on you today" (Deut.
6:5-6). We note the repetition here of the key word
"today".

    This God speaking his holy will anew to each of us
today and loved with all our heart, is closer to us than
any other god is to its devotees. The Lord then is closer
to us than any other supreme value in life, including life
itself. Not only our life but also the land where we live
has been given to us by the Lord "that you may live and

may enter in and take possession of the land which the Lord, the God of your fathers, is giving you."

Jesus turned spontaneously to the book of Deuteronomy. It was among his favorites, first because both he and this book originated in the northern part of the Promised Land, second because of Deuteronomy's sense of compassion and devotion *this day*. Whether in the temptation scene (Matt 4:1-11) or in answering the questions about the first and greatest law (Mark 12:28-34), Jesus replied with the words of this book.

Deuteronomy resonated the attitude of Jesus; it spoke to his best self more easily than many other books in the Bible. In this light we can appreciate Jesus' reflection: "Do not think that I have come to abolish the law and the prophets, but to fulfill them . . . not the smallest part of a letter of the law shall be done away with until it all comes true."

We, too, want to grow into this attitude of Jesus, modeled upon Deuteronomy. Lent is such a time of spiritual purification, so that the least wish of God becomes an absolute command for us. God in Jesus is that close to us. He speaks today, this moment. He appeals to the love of all our heart. Love such as this, stirred within our heart by God's immediate presence, happily takes away our liberty as we spontaneously seek this clasp of love. Without deciding between a million and one options we have chosen the very best, and all the world will testify: "This great nation is truly a wise and intelligent people."

> Glorify the Lord, O Jerusalem;
> praise your God, O Zion.
> For he has strengthened the bars of your gates;
> he has blessed your children within
> you.

Thursday — Third Week of Lent

Jer 7:23-28. Despite many prophets sent by God, still
the people do not listen to the voice of the Lord, their
God, or take correction.

Luke 11:14-23. Jesus casts out devils by the finger of
God . . . Whoever does not gather with Jesus scat-
ters.

While the passage from Jeremiah presents human
life in terms of a simple, obedient response to God,
Jesus' words in Luke's gospel recognize a violent struggle between devils and angels raging within us. Yet,
Jesus' exorcism, driving out the demon, made it possible for the man to speak, a power simply taken for
granted by the rest of us. In the same way, Jeremiah
declared the deadly seriousness about obedience to
God's will in the normal everyday details of life. Later
in the same chapter Jeremiah announced: "Beware!
days will come . . . when I will silence the cry of joy . . .
for the land will be turned to rubble" (Jer 7:32-34).

The simplest acts of basic human virtue — like
compassion, forgiveness, prayer, understanding, loy-
alty, loving affection — make all the difference between
heaven and hell, life and death, angelic or demonic
possession. At another place in Chapter seven Jeremiah
expressed it very clearly:

> Only if you thoroughly reform your ways
> and your deeds; if each of you deals
> justly with his neighbor, if you no
> longer oppress the resident alien, the
> orphan, and the widow; if you no longer
> shed innocent blood . . . or follow
> strange gods to your own harm will I
> [the Lord, your God] remain with you. (7:5-7)

Jesus, for his part, returned to this common sense style of response. He replied equivalently to his detractors: If I have done a very good act, how can you even suggest that I acted with an evil spirit? If I am compassionate towards a mute person, do not accuse me of sin! "If it is by the finger of God that I cast out devils, then the reign of God is upon you." The messianic age is at hand if we can speak kindly, love compassionately, protect courageously, receive even the alien warmheartedly.

Jeremiah and Jesus then do not differ as much as we supposed at first. Each sees a mighty struggle beneath simple human goodness; each announces a messianic kingdom within reach of everyone. The expectations seem so small compared to the extraordinary results. Jeremiah asked for a heart responsive to God's will, obedient to his laws of kindness and forgiveness. We must not be stiff-necked; we ought to be faithful, listening attentively and responsively.

Jeremiah's passage ends with the word "faithfulness." In the Hebrew language the word implies: *be what you are supposed to be!* It means consistency, fidelity. It expects people to act as their nature would normally act if evil never interfered. Yet, this consistency sets up a relationship with God, with *all* one's neighbors, even the alien in our midst, with angels and saints. Goodness ought to be as normal as breathing; to stop breathing spells death and demonic possession.

As we speak our simple "Amen! Thanks be to God!" to these biblical readings, we must resolve to be consistent. This Lent we must so help the needy and the stranger, that these virtuous actions become second nature to us. Then we will be acting under the finger of God and furthering the kingdom of God in our midst.

He is our God
>   and we are the people he shepherds
If today you hear his voice,
>   harden not your heart!

Friday—Third Week of Lent

Hos 14:2-10. Conclusion to the prophecy, calling Israel
to a prayerful, effective conversion.

Mark 12:28b-34. Jesus enunciates the first and second
greatest laws, love of God and love of one's neighbor.

These two Bible passages are cast in the style of
dialogue and offer an excellent example of praying or
studying the Sacred Scriptures. We are to consider not
only God or Jesus immediately present before us, but
the larger community of Israel or the Church also in our
group. The inspired authors—in today's reading they
are Hosea and Mark—add their own comments at the
end; after all, they edited or arranged the material.

In the prophecy of Hosea we take note of this series
of speakers:

Prophet Hosea or a priest: "Return, O Israel, to
the Lord, your God . . ."

Israel at prayer: "Forgive all iniquity . . ."

Israel in conversation: "Assyria will not save us,
. . . we shall say no more, 'Our God,' to the work of
our hands."

Israel at prayer: "In you [O Lord] the orphan finds
compassion."

God's reply: "I will heal their defection . . ."

Liturgical response: "He [Israel] shall strike root . . . Again they shall dwell in his [the Lord's] shade and raise grain . . ."

God's reply: "Ephraim! [another name for Israel] . . . I have humbled him but I will prosper him . . ."

Editor's comment: "Let him who is wise understand these things . . ."

Passages of the Bible like this one become a powerful instrument for prayer and for community discussion, because almost unconsciously a wide group of people are locked into practical discussion and profound prayer.

A different scenario of dialogue is seen in Mark's gospel yet the overall effect remains the same:

Setting: An argument between Jesus and some opponents.

Scribe: "Which is the first of all the commandments?"

Jesus: "Hear, O Israel! The Lord our God is Lord alone! Therefore, you shall love the Lord your God . . . love your neighbor as yourself."

Scribe: "Excellent, teacher! . . . love . . . is worth more than any burnt offering . . ."

Jesus: "You are not far from the reign of God."

Mark the Evangelist: "No one had the courage to ask him any more questions."

The thrust of each dialogue is conversion, but not necessarily restricted to a negative movement away from sin. In Hosea, Israel is to "return to the Lord, your God"; in Mark, one positively seeks love towards God and neighbor and thereby a proper love for oneself. This desire for God is a prayerful response, not a theoretical exposition. Rather than be distracted by the theology of conversion, the people reach out effectively with compassion for the orphan.

Each passage in its own way presents a healthy interchange with liturgical prayer. The scribe declares that love "is worth more than any burnt offering" and Hosea adds that once such love is secured then "we may render as offerings the bullocks from our stalls."

Both Hosea and Jesus speak in the language of the ancient Scriptures which they had learned from participating in the liturgy. Liturgical celebrations on earth reflect the beauty and peace of heavenly life. Heaven's dew, Hosea states, rests upon Israel. Jesus says "Amen" to this anticipation of heaven: "You are not far from the reign of God."

Hosea and Mark enable us to put all of our Lenten practices into proper relationship, each with the other, ourselves with our neighbor and Church, all with God.

If only my people would hear me,
and Israel walk in my ways,
I would feed them with the best of wheat,
and with honey from the rock I would
fill them.

Saturday—Third Week of Lent

Hos 5:15c-6:6. The people repeat a liturgical prayer as if it were a magic formula. The prophet replies that such blasphemy will destroy them.

Luke 18:9-14. The parable of the publican and the pharisee. The criterion of genuine prayer.

If we know our Bible very well, especially if we have memorized the sacred words, then we have a storeroom of statements for every occasion. We can muster the correct theological response and wrap a mantle of piety about us and so feel very holy, proper and self-righteous. Even the devil can quote the Holy Scripture, says Shakespeare; this corrupt demon can then appear as an angel of light! If a little learning is a dangerous thing, a great deal of learning about the Bible can be still more perilous. Bible study destroys us if it is not accompanied by fasting, alms-giving, sincere conversion of morals, humble prayer.

The certainty of God's answering our prayers was deeply imbedded within Israel's tradition; Jesus also repeats the same confidence. Hosea quotes the people's liturgical prayer: "Come, let us return to the Lord, . . . He will revive us after two days; on the third day he will raise us up." This theme of salvation on the third day occurs frequently enough in the Old Testament (Gen 42:18; Ex 19:10-11; Josh 3:2; Hos 6:2; Jon 2:1; Ezr 8:15; Esth 5:1; Luke 13:32). Jesus confirms this outstanding biblical symbol by rising from the dead "on the third day."

God certainly answers prayers, but he can be angered by our mouthing of words. For words to become true prayer, it is not enough that they be consecrated by a sacred tradition and employed in a holy setting. Words are transformed into prayer, says the prophet Hosea, by love and the knowledge of God.

In other parts of his prophecy Hosea explained what he expects these two phrases, "love" and "knowledge of God," to mean for us, They dispel "false swearing, lying, murder, stealing and adultery" (Hos 4:1-2). When love, on the contrary, is genuine, it exemplifies the deeper meaning of its Hebrew root, *hesed*. Such love is basically the spontaneous and therefore obligatory response of common blood and family bond. In Israel's culture *hesed* existed only in a family or clan or tribe, never between strangers or foreigners. When God declared himself a kinsman or blood relative of Israel, then the bond of such relationship was rooted in God. *All* equally belonged to God and consequently to one another's family.

For these reasons the words of the Bible sprang from the depth of such an intimate relationship between Israel and the Lord. Israel's words became inspired with God's life, ideals and response, because her words were born of a relationship or union between God and Israel.

Now we understand, first why every prayer is heard, for it springs from the common life or "blood" shared by Israel and God. But we ought to comprehend as well why such words can destroy. To mouth such words from a heart separated from God and from one's neighbor is to make use of intimate symbols like a kiss or a caress to mock and to betray.

Where love, however, is deep, and its expression genuine, then it is characterized by exquisite wonder, awesome fear, humble unworthiness, delicate concern over the least infraction. It does not brag for it never does enough. Such a person, Jesus tells us, is the publican. The pharisee's piety, on the contrary, is a "morning cloud." It looks glorious and heavenly, but it is flimsy and it evaporates quickly. Because it looked good, it pretends to be good. It has destroyed reality. Because the roots of *hesed* are deep, there is still hope.

> It is steadfast love, not sacrifice,
>> that God desires.
> My sacrifice, O God, is a contrite spirit;
>> A heart contrite and humbled, O God,
>> you will not spurn.

FOURTH WEEK OF LENT

Monday — Fourth Week of Lent

Is 65:17-21. God creates new heavens and a new earth, and in the new Jerusalem no longer shall the sound of weeping be heard.

John 4:43-54. Jesus has arrived in Galilee where the people welcomed him because of his miracles. At Capernaum Jesus responded to the faith of a royal official by curing his son — "the second sign."

Through the prophet Isaiah God promises us "new heavens and a new earth." We look forward to a vibrant life, fresher than just the old made new. It will be a new creation, a total transformation. Although we ourselves and everyone else will be the same persons who lived on the old planet earth, nonetheless this line of continuity will lead into a heavenly existence so marvelous that "the things of the past shall not be remembered . . . No longer shall the sounds of weeping be heard there."

Jesus promised a similar vision to the royal official at Capernaum. "His son . . . was near death. He begged Jesus 'to come down and restore the boy to health' . . . Jesus told him, 'return home. Your son will live.' " This pagan official of Roman origin "put his trust in . . . Jesus . . . and started for home." He believed that the boy whom he had last seen "near death" will now meet him full of life!

Do we walk through life vibrating the hope and confidence of this pagan official? Do we believe that Jesus can, if he will, work miracles in our lives? Are we convinced that Jesus lovingly cares for each member of our family and neighborhood whatever be his religion or origin? Can we honestly admit that our heart is secure in its faith, that whatever happens at the end of each project or journey, was really and truly the very best—no matter what? If we find sickness and death, do we say in our heart: "Jesus could have cured this person or could have arranged this business differently, so if he left it this way, it is the very best. I believe, Lord."

If the tears are not yet wiped away and the sound of crying is still heard, then the suffering and loss are a manifestation of persevering love and courageous dedication, on God's part who sorrows with the sorrowing, on our part who rally around for comfort and support. "We believe, Lord. Even in this agony you give us a vision of new heavens and a new earth! We will live through death in this hope."

We also believe that had Jesus wanted to do so, he would have worked a miracle for us. If he did not, we are not angered or frustrated. We are all the more convinced that pain is directly willed by God as it was appointed for Jesus on the cross.

Jesus can work miracles. The centurion believed Jesus, "Your son will live." Anyone who passed this pagan Roman on his way home must have been startled by the brilliant hope in his eyes, the enthusiasm for life in his gait, the special swing of his body. Do people who pass us by, perceive something about us specially hopeful and joyfully optimistic? They certainly should, for we, too, have seen a vision of "new heavens and a new earth."

Faith such as this does not destroy human initiative. If it did, the royal official never would have bothered coming to Jesus nor asked that his son continue to live, work, love and grow old.

Jesus, the gospel concludes, performed "this . . .

second sign." The miracle of turning water into wine at
Cana was the first sign (John 2:11). These are signs of
new life and new joy, miraculously achieved, so wonderful that the old things must be swept away and "the
past . . . not be remembered." If they are signs of death,
these signs point to a new creation through and beyond
death.

> Hear, O Lord, and have pity on me;
> You changed my mourning into dancing;
> > O Lord, my God, forever will I give
> > you thanks.

Tuesday — Fourth Week of Lent

Ez 47:1-9. A stream of fresh water originates from the
    Holy of Holies at the Jerusalem temple and miracu-
    lously transforms the desert into tropical vegetation;
    the Dead Sea turns into fresh water.

John 5:1-3a, 5-16. The cure of the lame man, on the
    Sabbath at the pool of Bethesda.

We live in an age of pollution and crisis. Our air and
our water are becoming so seriously contaminated that
we are approaching an alarming crisis. The fresh-water
image, therefore, in the prophecy of Ezekiel has all the
more appeal to us; its miraculous origin all the more
necessary. Only by an act of God, it seems, can the
destruction of our planet be reversed. Ezekiel offers us
reasons to hope and pray.

In the meanwhile Ezekiel inspires us to pray and
work for another, closer kind of purification, that of
ourselves. Each of us needs a stream of fresh water to
flow through us, to wash and invigorate our minds and

hearts, to bring a new fresh vigor to our attitudes, to enliven and brighten our hopes, to allow a new spontaneity within our reflexes. Each of us is only half or a quarter alive; we are lame like the man in John's gospel, waiting for the movement of the water.

While Lent is a period of penance and self-denial—seemingly a time of dull oppression beneath grey cloudy skies—it also recalls the waters of Baptism. It is a period for preparing catechumens for the sacrament of Baptism on Holy Saturday. Lent trains us like athletes, to throw off the sluggish and heavy drag of gloom and pessimism. It keeps away false values, so that our best self emerges fully alive.

The waters of Ezekiel's prophecy flow from the Holy of Holies at the temple. We are reminded of the sanctuary of our parish churches where we are summoned more frequently during Lent. Through added prayer and instruction at the *liturgy* we feel the touch of these transforming waters. The larger or complete passage of Ezekiel (verses one to twelve) show that the prophet is meditating upon earlier biblical passages, especially one in Jer 17:5-7. Reflecting upon the Bible we are provided with another source of life-giving, invigorating water; like Ezekiel we will be more able to spot new signs of life about us where previously we saw only desert.

This spirit of optimism will increase more and more as we spend more time in prayer, reflection and dialogue. These more extended periods are indicated by Ezekiel as the angel of the Lord led the prophet along the route of the stream of fresh water, and at each new thousand cubits the water was continuously deeper. The possibilities of new life are increased as the Bible purifies our vision through the example of the saints and

strengthens our faith not only in miracles but also in
ourselves and in our neighbor.

Finally, the lame man at the pool of Bethesda advises us to *wait*. This most important virtue is incul-
cated by the prophets, especially by Isaiah who said:
"By waiting and by calm you shall be saved, in quiet and
in trust your strength lies" (Is 30:15). Waiting convinces
ourselves and all others that Jesus alone, certainly not
our activity without Jesus, works the transforming, at
times miraculous change we need. The lame man could
have waited forever and remained lame unless waiting
prepared a vigilant spirit for the coming of Jesus.

> There is a stream whose runlets gladden the
>   city of God,
>   the holy dwelling of the Most High.
> God is in its midst; it shall not be disturbed;
>   God will help it at the break of dawn.

Wednesday—Fourth Week of Lent

Is 49:8-15. A medley of themes from Second Isaiah,
author of ch 40-55: suffering servant (v 8-9a), new
exodus (v 9b-12), comfort across heaven and earth (v
13), tenderness for mother Zion (v 14-15).

John 5:17-30. In this meditation on life Jesus' enemies
are working to destroy him, even on the Sabbath,
because Jesus *worked* a life-giving miracle on the
Sabbath!

The biblical readings from Isaiah chapters 40 to 55
(a distinct section of the prophecy, dating to the
Babylonian exile) and from the gospel of John over-
whelm us with many manifestations of tenderness and

might. The heaven and earth sing out their wondrous enthusiasm at the Lord's splitting the mountains to bring his people from afar. Almost in the same breath the prophet sees this mighty God as a mother with tender love for the child of her womb. The images clash from our human viewpoint but serve to enhance the *mystery* of God.

John's gospel moves in and out of the most profound mysteries of the Godhead. This passage returns repeatedly to the equality of Father and Son in the Holy Trinity as well as to the subordination of Jesus, the God-man, to the Father. Questions about life and death, judgment and resurrection, sin and grace, heaven and damnation, life received and life possessed, all these mystical phenomena rise to the surface of John's gospel here.

Such indeed are the tremendous possibilities of our own life. We can be so deeply touched by tender, exquisite joy that we summon the distant mountains to "break forth in song." We feel very helpless, even condemned by our sins, yet at the same time these sins evoke the concern of our Savior-God, who is "saying to the prisoners: 'Come out!' [and] to those in darkness: 'Show yourselves!' "

The depth of goodness and the height of power, the plunging into the eternity behind us and the sweep of contemplation into another future eternity—all this leaves us in awe.

All the while people are arguing whether or not Jesus should work miracles on the Sabbath. He has performed the miracle of curing the lame person at the pool of Bethesda, and jealous people bicker over a violation of Sabbath rest. Already in another passage the prophecy of Isaiah explained how to "keep the

Sabbath free from profanation": "do what is just . . . and let the foreigners join themselves to the Lord" (Is 56:1-8). God the Father works on the Sabbath by keeping the created world in good running condition, by bringing infants to birth and by calling others in death. Yet, people allow themselves to be blind to the wonderful and the tender, to argue a miniscule point of legal procedure. A tiny hill turns into a mountain to block the view of God's beautiful world of people and natural phenomena.

We, too, can become narrow, prejudiced, blinded. We can become absorbed in all types of red tape as the poor die of starvation, the handicapped are deprived of a full life, and the excitement of a younger person is smothered.

We can also hide ourselves in darkness, fearful about the wonder of life. To inhabit a world of miracles and of healing, of mountains split apart and breaking into song, of lengthy contemplations of eternal life— these actions can be so overwhelming that we cannot endure them for long. We want to be distracted; we allow every small annoyance to bring us back to our own tiny bit of reality.

Lent ought to purify and strengthen our gaze, so that we can live magnanimously with the wonderful person of God, with the awesome gift of life, and with the good planet earth.

> The Lord is faithful in all his words
> > and holy in all his works.
> The Lord lifts up all who are falling
> > and raises up all who are bowed
> > down.

Thursday—Fourth Week of Lent

Ex 32:7-14. When God protests that he will destroy the Israelites and raise up a new people in Moses, Moses prays, invoking God's promises to the Patriarchs as well as the ridicule of the other nations.

John 5:31-47. Jesus argues with his opponents who do not accept him. Jesus appeals to the witness of: a) John the Baptist; b) the miracles; c) the Father's presence; and d) the Scriptures. Each person will be judged by his background and opportunity; Jesus' opponents, therefore, by Moses.

The biblical readings center around complaints and responses. Since criticism is a very human reaction, we should all feel very much at home!

God complains to Moses about the people Israel: "See how stiff-necked!" In fact God wants to quit this community and start a new chosen nation in Moses and his sons. "I will make you a great nation." All of us condemn quitters; yet if we are really honest, each one of us is *tempted* to quit at times of crisis.

In regard to the episode here, the question comes to mind: is Moses projecting *his own* problem into the mind of God? Moses had hesitated at other times, especially when he balked at striking the rock for water and then in doubt did it twice (Num 20:6b-13). If Moses is confusing his own temptation with God's, then we have a true brother or identical twin in Moses. Like Moses we, too, imagine at times that our temptation to quit is actually an expression of God's holy will!

A major temptation of all leaders, and indeed of each one of us because of our very special unique gifts, is to run *ahead* of our community or church. We feel that it is God's will to leave behind the slow, dull, sinful lot of other people, so that we can be true to our conscience, full in expressing our hopes, at peace with our ideals. Such temptations are very human, but to give in not only separates us from our community or church but it also pulls us away from Moses and Jesus.

Jesus in the footsteps of Moses and the prophets, argued seriously and continuously, even though he had just healed a cripple and helped a man lame for 38 years to walk. Surely, if anyone of us had displayed such divine power out of compassion for the handicapped, we would hardly be in the mood to enter a long discussion—first about the legal niceties of our actions (should we have done a good deed on the Sabbath?— 5:1-30); and then about the presence of God supporting our miraculous action.

Both Jesus and the early church patiently "sat down" and carefully worked through the various reasons. This response is not to be attributed to condescension but to compassion and genuine love. Jesus appealed to the recent experience of John the Baptist, again to his own miracles as works of his heavenly Father, to the interior presence of God the Father within the mind of each person, and to the Scriptures.

We must decide, during a lively discussion or argument, which approach is best. Perhaps, the least probative and argumentative, the weakest in the face of opposition, yet the most genuine and in the long run the most powerful reason is found in God's hidden presence, his "silent" testimony on our behalf. Our first decision, our consequent action, our present reappraisal should be undertaken in God's presence. As Jeremiah expressed it: I have "stood in the council of the Lord to see and hear his word" (Jer 23:18).

This interior conviction, borne and sustained by

our consciousness of living with God and of being directed by the Lord, will *eventually* overcome all opposition and win the argument. This attitude of serenity enables us to persevere and thus remove the temptation to quit and so to enable this community eventually, perhaps in the next generation as in Moses' case, to cross the river Jordan and enter the promised land. We do not seek to win an argument but a people for God.

Lord, remember us,
for the love you bear your people.

Friday — Fourth Week of Lent

Wis 2:1, 12-22. The wicked test the patience of the just person and the fidelity of God to deliver the oppressed.

John 7:1-2, 10, 25-30. Jesus traveled privately to Jerusalem for the feast of Tabernacles. While he preached publicly, he affirmed the mysterious privacy or secret of his origin.

The "just one" in the first reading, persecuted and tested by the wicked, annoys others and seems to provoke this oppression because "he professes to have knowledge of God and styles himself a child of God." A similar, mysterious origin is claimed by Jesus. When the men and women of his own relation claimed to have all the facts on Jesus, he replied: "I was sent by One whom . . . you do not know. I know him because it is from him I come." While the "just one" in the Book of Wisdom is humiliated and oppressed, "no one laid a finger on . . . [Jesus] because his hour had not yet come."

At the depth of each person, then, is a mysterious

life, not only created by God but also directed by the Lord at each "hour." There is an hour of peace and an hour of violence, an hour of birth and an hour of re-birth into eternity. Just as death and immortality are wondrously absorbed in God's infinite knowledge and loving care, so also is the birth, the inner character and temperament, the sequence of life. These most essential parts of our person, these most crucial moments of our existence are all locked in the secrecy of God's divine life. Not even we ourselves can ever properly and fully comprehend who we really are at the roots of our soul, and we will be perpetually taken by surprise even at critical moments of our lives. Shall we say, especially at these decisive crossroads will we react with undreamed of strength, wisdom and holiness?

Temptations and trials result when people and forces from outside attempt to invade this mysterious domain of God, to force us to mediocre compromises, to catch us in selfish and harmful plots, to contrive ways of misusing God's beautiful creation against his other children, to use power and prestige for improper or self-indulgent projects, to make everyone the same by removing all signs of heroic dedication. What the Book of Wisdom recounts about temptation and persecution from the wicked can be said of enemy forces outside each of us and at times from within ourselves where these forces of evil have been lodged.

These forces cannot always be fought directly and on their own terms. We need an exceptional amount of hidden resources and personal strength. Lent provides an opportunity to contact our finest, divinely created and most mysterious self. Lent enables us to retrace our steps back to our roots. Our spirit can rest more profoundly and more continuously at the base of ourselves through the extended periods of prayer and frequent summons to penance in this holy time of the year. Fasting purifies and strengthens, removes the false values and easy traps to selfishness and sensuality. Alms-giving unites us with brothers and sisters whom we meet only in that depth of life where everyone is equally created by God as one marvelous family. Prayer takes on the patient and quiet attitude of resting with one's beloved, who is God. It listens to the "hidden counsels of God."

At the response after the first reading we confess: "The Lord is near to broken hearts." Broken hearts are painful and lonely, but they also enable us to reach even more deeply into our roots, where God is very near with the loving providence of his mysterious clasp.

> The Lord is close to the brokenhearted;
> > and those who are crushed in spirit
> > he saves
> Many are the troubles of the just man,
> > but out of them all the Lord delivers
> > him.

Saturday—Fourth Week of Lent

Jer 11:18-20. With his life threatened by his own relatives, Jeremiah confided his cause to the Lord.

John 7:40-53. Disputes arise among the people, whether or not Jesus is the messiah. The Sanhedrin acts as though they can decide the question even without a hearing.

The biblical authorities in the days of Jesus are undecided about him. The majority conclude from the

Bible that Jesus is not the promised Savior and Prophet. The same scriptural argument raged among the lay people, yet a strange group of them decided in Jesus' favor. The temple guards responded the most spontaneously of all: "No one ever spoke like that before!"

In our day many leading Christians, theologians and large numbers of lay people argue among themselves over the essentials of religion: who is Christ? What is the Church? What is necessary for salvation? What is right and wrong? Even Christianity itself is divided, at this moment anyway, into irreconcilable denominations, each quoting the Bible!

Because Lent summons us to more extended prayer and study, to a daily Eucharistic celebration with special biblical readings, we need to review the norms for reading the Bible profitably. Today's selections from the prophecy of Jeremiah and the gospel of John offer some help for interpreting the Bible more correctly today.

First, as Nicodemus pointed out, we should give the Bible and each person a fair hearing; we should try to know the facts before we condemn or accept. As we make this studious effort at study and patient observation, we will have to tolerate differences of opinion. If indecision about Jesus' messiahship became a public issue both among the people themselves and among religious authorities, even while Jesus was still alive, then we ought not be surprised about theological conflicts today.

At the same time we should be careful about quickly taking sides to change. It should be noted that Jesus gave no indication that he or his disciples should change and abandon the Jewish religion. The controversy raged around the way in which God should bring this religion to greater perfection.

Another quality important for Bible study in terms of contemporary life, is a healthy respect for whatever is good and wholesome. The unlearned temple guards reply to the court theologians: "No one ever spoke like that before!" The Bible ought never be used to make the good look bad; rather, the real task of biblical interpretation lies in making the good to be still better.

Negative answers are more likely to be wrong; positive explanations more likely to be correct. Good, wholesome people, positive in affirming others, slow to condemn, ready to forgive, tolerant of other people's convictions, prayerful and respectful, have the best chance of being right.

Both Jeremiah and Jesus interpreted the Bible within the context of their religious community. Each presumed a living continuity with past tradition, each sought an understanding of the Bible within the hopes and prayers of their contemporary "church" or assembly of believers. Bible study was not a matter settled exclusively between each individual and God. One's family and entire nation were seriously involved and a true answer is found only where unity prevails.

Finally, in such a dispute, Jeremiah entrusted his cause to the Lord, "searcher of mind and heart." Above all, we are not seeking answers but the living God; we are not settling disputes but responding to God's loving, searching presence within us. Only when we peacefully seek God rather than ammunition for religious disputes will we be in good shape to interpret the Bible correctly.

O Lord, my God, in you I take refuge;
> save me from all my pursuers and
> rescue me,

Lest I become like the lion's prey,
> to be torn to pieces, with no one to
> rescue me.

FIFTH WEEK OF LENT

Monday—Fifth Week of Lent

Dan 13:1-9, 15-17, 19-30, 33-62. Story of chaste Susanna, who refused to sin even at the threat of disgrace and death and was saved by God.

John 8:1-11. Jesus protects the woman caught in adultery by asking the one without sin to be the first to cast a stone at her.

Or

John 8:12-20. Jesus is the light of the world. His and the Father's witness provide a double guarantee.

These three biblical passages reflect secret moments in all our lives: moments when we are suspected of evil and helpless to properly explain ourselves; or other moments when we are guilty and never allowed to forget it by our accusers; or still other moments when we are convinced before God about the goodness of some other person and yet remain incapable of expressing ourselves adequately before a skeptical crowd.

The key to survival lies in the one line about Susanna: "Through her tears she looked up to heaven, for she trusted in the Lord wholeheartedly." By contrast the Bible states that the two wicked men, her accusers, "suppressed their consciences; they would not allow their eyes to look to heaven." When we fix our gaze on heaven, we allow ourselves to be wholly absorbed in God and from this intense union we acquire an extraordinary peace and unconquerable strength. This peace is Christ's "farewell gift," given not as the world bestows peace, but infused far more profoundly into our lives.

This peace begets an exceptional kind of patience.

Jesus' words come to mind, especially as they used to ring out in the ancient Latin liturgy, *in patientia vestra possidebitis animas vestras*, translated literally "in your patience you will possess your soul" (Luke 21:10). In such a spirit Susanna turned immediately to the Lord and prayed: "O Eternal God, you know what is hidden and are aware of all things. . . ." She did not lash out angrily against her accusers, nor did she turn at once in panic to her own defense. She looked to the Lord, and in this patience she possessed her strength and integrity. Rather than fall into the trap of arguing when her accusers were crafty, she forced everyone to come up to her innocence and honesty before God.

We are directed first to remember God's presence and his sweeping knowledge of everything and then to abide in prayer. In this way our own defense does not turn into a shouting match where nobody wins and we ourselves lose our own innocence in this excessive form of revenge and counterattack.

The guilty woman in John's gospel, lay silently at Jesus' feet. Again we admire Jesus' as well as the woman's restraint. He "simply bent down and started tracing [and doodling] on the ground with his finger. . . . [Finally] he straightened up and said to them, 'Let the man among you who has no sin be the first to cast a stone at her.' A second time he bent down and wrote on the ground." She might have shouted accusations against the man who must have been caught in the act with her and yet was allowed to slip away easily. Her accusers did not want justice. Otherwise both culprits would have been brought to Jesus. They were using the woman to trap Jesus.

Jesus refused to be trapped, and so did the woman whose silence against the ground projected far more

honor and dignity than the tall, self-justifying pompos-
ity of the accusers. They eventually "drifted away one
by one beginning with the elders."

We pray for the wisdom to know when to choose
that silence which begets honor, serenity, forgiveness.
These beautiful mysterious depths of character come
when we possess our soul in the presence of Jesus. He
becomes our light, our witness, our justification. Jesus,
a new Daniel, enables not just ourselves but an ever
wider circle of our neighbors to pray, "blessing God
who saves those who hope in him."

> Though I walk in the dark valley
> > I fear no evil; for you are at my side
> With your rod and your staff
> > that give me courage.

Tuesday—Fifth Week of Lent

Num 21:4-9. Moses lifted up a bronze serpent, symbol
of the people's sins and the instrument of their salvation.

John 8:21-30. Jesus will be lifted up by the people Israel
and then they will realize that he is the "I Am" of their
tradition, one with the God Yahweh.

The Bible readings insist that as a family or community we admit who we are, what we have done, and
what we hope to be, honestly and openly before God
and before one another. This confession is our only way
to life, not to say, survival; to suppress this truth will
encase a destructive force within us.

The symbol of Israel's sin, the saraph serpent (the
Hebrew word "saraph" means "burning"), sent among

them with a poisonous bite, is transformed into an instrument of salvation. Moses made a bronze serpent and mounted it on a pole, so that all who look upon it with an honest admission of their sin and sincere sorrow for their offense, will be forgiven and cured by the Lord. Such an acknowledgment purifies the mind and heart, for it exposes and eliminates all false reasons and phony excuses and calls the evil action by its right name "sin". The people admit that their sin brought sorrow and death, that their grumbling was destructive, and that their waste of food or contempt for it evoked God's righteous anger.

This bronze serpent had a somewhat devious history. Long before Moses cast this figure out of copper, the serpent was a popular idol or figurine in the Canaanite fertility ritual. It is to be noted that the serpent symbolized the devil in Genesis chapter 3. Perhaps it was partially because of this pagan background that Moses' bronze serpent became an object of false worship. It was, therefore, smashed and destroyed by King Hezekiah (2 Kgs 18:4).

Strange it is that the early church recognized in this symbol a sign of Jesus on the cross. Jesus crucified shows the full effects of *our* sins. *Jesus has become ourselves* in our most destructive and violent actions. Jesus *is* ourselves, our families and communities, jealous and hateful one against the other, resentful and prejudiced. Jesus thus becomes one with us even in our sins and guilt; yet all the while he preserves his goodness, peace and godliness.

St. Paul wrote: "For our sakes God made him [Jesus] who did not know sin, *to be sin*, so that in him we might become the very holiness of God" (2 Cor 5:21). In the goodness, compassion, mercy, tenderness, forgiveness of Jesus we recognize at once *by contrast* our own violent and harsh attitude. This same image of Jesus on the cross not only portrays our personal and community violence, but it also reveals "the kindness and love of God our Savior" (Tit 3:4).

Like the saraph serpent, lifted up by Moses, likewise Jesus crucified, lifted up by our sins and those of all the world, "trains us to reject godless ways and worldly desires . . . as we await our blessed hope . . . our Savior Christ Jesus. It was he who sacrificed himself for us . . . [and by submerging his goodness within us] redeem[ed] us from all unrighteousness and . . . cleansed for himself a people of his own, eager to do what is right" (Tit 2:12-14).

While externally Jesus conforms to us, internally we are able to conform to him. This internal goodness forces the poison of our sinfulness out of us—in the violent and hideous form of crucifixion—and at that moment we like Jesus belong to what is above.

O Lord, hear my prayer,
And let my cry come to you.

Wednesday—Fifth Week of Lent

Dan 3:14-20, 91-92, 95. The young men submit to a fiery furnace, regardless of the consequences, rather than put anyone in place of God.

John 8:31-42. Like Jesus, the true offspring of Abraham lives by faith, doing whatever be the will of God and believing always in God's promises.

The young men in the book of Daniel obediently follow their consciences and believe in God no matter what happens: "If our God . . . can save us . . ., may he save us! But even if he will not, know, O king, that we will not serve your god . . ." With unimaginable serenity they accept the consequences. "There is no need," they said, "for us to defend ourselves." The issue is very clear; there is no other choice but what is alone morally good and acceptable, even obligatory.

God saved them from being consumed in the "furnace . . . heated seven times more than usual." Nebuchadnezzar then exclaimed: "Blessed be the God . . . who sent his angel to deliver the servants that trusted in him."

Jesus, too, did always "the will of him who sent me" (John 5:30). That is why Jesus declared: "I have come down from heaven, but to do the will of him who sent me" (6:38). Such heroic obedience was "my food" (4:34). Yet, unlike the young men in the fiery furnace, Jesus was not saved from the violent death of crucifixion.

Such a death, nonetheless, was the answer to his prayers. As contradictory as this seems, such is the explanation of Jesus' agony in the garden offered to us in the Epistle to the Hebrews!

> In the days when he was in the flesh, he offered prayers and supplications with loud cries and tears to God, who was able to save him from death, and he was heard because of his reverence. Son though he was, he learned obedience from what he suffered; and when perfected he became the source of eternal salvation for all who obey him. (Hebr 5:7-9)

By such obedience Jesus manifests his divine sonship. "I did not come of my own will; it was he who sent me." Jesus' eternal life in the unity of the Holy Trinity consisted in being continuously begotten by the Father. His response, "I obey" constituted his essential life, his "I Am". He had no other claim to existence.

The whole existence of ourselves as disciples of Jesus flows from the mysterious roots of our souls where we are called and sustained in a supernatural life beyond all human ability to comprehend. Jesus said in today's gospel:

> If you live according to my teaching,
> you are truly my disciples;
> then you will know the truth,
> and the truth will set you free.

Although we must make many decisions from our own conscious intelligence and we must act according to our talents and opportunities, nonetheless, at the base or core of ourselves we are being begotten by God and we are receiving a divine life similar to Jesus. At crucial moments in our lives we are expected to be heroic. In fact we have no other choice. Neither did the young men in the book of Daniel. Nothing may interfere with what is morally good. "The truths [of that deep, divine life] will set you free."

As we respond with fearless obedience, that most divine part of ourselves is manifest. Our true self emerges most fully, most courageously, most divinely. If as in the case of Jesus our prayer to be saved is heard through the act of dying, we are saved for eternal life, and the angels will exclaim: "Blessed be the God . . . who sent his angels to deliver the servants who trusted in him."

Blessed are you, O Lord, the God of our
            fathers,
                praiseworthy and exalted above all
                forever;
And blessed is your holy and glorious name,
                praiseworthy and exalted above all
                for all ages.

Thursday—Fifth Week of Lent

Gen 17:3-9. God changes Abram's name to Abraham
    and promises to make him the father of many nations.
John 8:51-59. Jesus says that "Abraham rejoiced to see
    my day." In fact, Jesus added: "Before Abraham
    came to be, I AM."

The promises of Abraham reach forward, even into
the centuries beyond our present age. In speaking to
Abraham God anticipated a day when all the nations of
the world will find themselves united as though they
were blood-relatives, all of them offspring of their one
father Abraham. The different races of planet earth and
the various ethnic groups cannot establish this bond
through a common genealogy or blood descent. It can
happen only by sharing the same faith and hopes and
that means faith in land promised equally to all persons,
faith in a way of salvation where no single group travels
alone, faith in a common sharing of earth's riches, faith
in the one divine dignity of all persons.

The choice of Abraham, when compared to the
later exodus out of Egypt under Moses, has a much
more universal sweep to it. It reflects the kingdom of
David when Israel opened lively diplomatic relations on
an international scale and absorbed many customs and

values of their neighbors—with God's blessing. God's promises to Abraham advise us to think big, to respond openly, to seek and dream the divine ideal of one world, one people.

While Abraham looks ahead excitedly, the words of Jesus reach back not only to the age of the great patriarch (1850 B.C.) but even behind that first day in Israel's history to the eternal day before creation. "Before Abraham came to be, I AM." Jesus identifies himself with Yahweh. This name for God, very special and sacred to Israel, means in the Hebrew language "He who is always there."

Jesus, consequently, claims to be more than the fulfillment of Abraham's faith and hopes; Jesus is one with God who planned for the day of Abraham before the universe was created, directed world history so that Abraham would be the single hope of all people, led Israel's history forward till this eternal Word became incarnate as Jesus, son of Mary.

Jesus, as the great I AM, is the Lord of our history. The hopes and plans of Jesus will remain at least partially unfulfilled until all men and women are one. We are reminded of St. Paul's famous statement:

> All of you who have been baptized into Christ have clothed yourselves with him. There does not exist among you Jew or Greek, slave or free person, male or female. All are one in Christ Jesus. Furthermore, if you belong to Christ, you are the descendants of Abraham, which means you inherit all that was promised. (Gal 3:27-29)

This Lent it is the duty of each of us to see that Abraham can rejoice even more abundantly to see Jesus' day *now*. The heart of father Abraham will beat with greater satisfaction to the extent that each of us breaks down barriers of prejudice and bias, of antagonism and refusal to forgive. Abraham will be even happier as each of us and our church across the world, champions the rights of oppressed people, people neglected in hospitals, rest homes and prisons.

Charity such as that benefits from the promise of Jesus: "if anyone is true to my word, that person shall never see death." Charity cannot die. It surpasses faith and hope and alone extends into heaven. The bond of love promised in Abraham, fulfilled in Jesus, summons us to the only way we can live forever.

The cycle is complete—from Jesus the great I AM before creation, through Abraham, to Jesus born in time of Abraham's stock, to ourselves for all eternity.

> You descendants of Abraham, his servants,
>> sons of Jacob, his chosen ones!
> He the Lord is our God;
>> throughout the earth his judgments
>> prevail.

Friday—Fifth Week of Lent

Jer 20:10-13. Surrounded by false friends who seek to entrap him, Jeremiah confided himself to the Lord, "you who test the just, who probe mind and heart."

John 10:31-42. Confronted by his adversaries who argue from the Bible, Jesus shows that he too can answer from the Bible, but he rested his case with his good works. He rested his own spirit in "the Father [who] is in me and I in him."

Both the prophet Jeremiah and the prophet Jesus

are hounded by friends and even relatives who have turned against them. These erstwhile, fair weather companions feel betrayed by Jeremiah or Jesus in that their own personal interests and selfish security are threatened. Jeremiah speaks of "the Lord [who] . . . has rescued the life of the poor" and Jesus cures the helpless—the blind and the crippled, the deaf and the mute—and returns them to full vigor on the Sabbath day. Each is condemned because each is upsetting the comfortable, legal support-system and shifting concern from red-tape to people.

In all honesty we must admit that the opposition group arguing against Jeremiah and Jesus are not openly bad people. They even know their Bible and its legal applications; they can quote all of them by rote memory. Yet these had become just sounds, no longer meaningful words.

These words had become sacred because they grew out of the living context of life, out of the hearts where people struggled to discern God's will in difficult or challenging moments of their life. These words then expressed so well that inner wrestling with God that later generations repeated them over and over again. Through these sacred writings the future assemblies were able to discern better God's wonderful but mysterious action in their own lives; this enabled them to respond more clearly and energetically to what God was asking.

These sacred words are so good that they can become idols worshipped in place of God. They can be quoted to control God and to dictate how God must act forever in the future. These practitioners of religion can then safeguard their own sanctimonious security which is now untouchable.

All of us can fall into this trap. We can be caught by our own goodness. Our virtue erects a castle of pride which becomes the home of the devil. Jesus condemned this fearful, desperate situation when he compared these people to "white-washed tombs, beautiful to look at on the outside but inside full of filth and dead men's bones" (Matt 23:27). Their actions are begotten by their "father [whom] you spring from, . . . the devil" (John 8:44).

This dreadful situation emerges whenever we "use" our goodness selfishly to our own advantage, insensitively against others. All of us commit our "best" sins when we are capable, talented, gifted and blessed by God. We use our God-given faculties in a wrong way. The worst of all these sins is pride when we seek to manipulate God to our egotistic plans; we do this by using our virtue to force others, even the Lord, into our self-centered way of life.

We can correct and avoid this evil tendency lurking in all of us "good" people, first by an outgoing, common-sense, delicate sensitivity towards the needs of others. Then we must root ourselves in God. Jeremiah turns to the Lord, "you who test the good, who probe mind and heart." Jesus allows his spirit to sink into the source of his eternal existence, "the Father [who] is in me and I in him."

We must repeat with the apostle Thomas, "My Lord and my God" (John 20:28), with Peter, "Lord, to whom shall we go? You have the words of eternal life" (John 6:68), or with today's antiphon after the reading of Jeremiah:

> In my distress I called upon the Lord,
> and he heard me.

Saturday—Fifth Week of Lent

Ez 37:21-28. Ezekiel announces one people, one land, one prince, one sanctuary forever.

John 11:45-57. As the high priest Caiphas "prophesized" that "one man die" for the people, the evangelist adds: "Not for this nation [of Israel] only, but to gather into one all the dispersed children of God."

In order that "all the dispersed children of God" lock hands and hearts and become one family as the prophet Ezekiel announced, they are not being asked to lose anything at all. Many centuries after Ezekiel prophesized, the apostle St. Paul told the gentile or pagan converts to "ponder and preserve all that is true . . . , honest, pure, admirable, decent, virtuous or worthy of praise." (Phil 4:8). These God-given talents and qualities, however, must be *shared* and thereby further enriched in "a covenant of peace . . . an everlasting covenant" of God's people among themselves and with their God.

"To share the best" is the rub of the matter. No one of us sweats too much over sharing our superfluous items. In fact we are anxious to clean house, give them away, and forget about them. But the Bible does not want us simply to get rid of things; such an action runs the risk of being pompous, altruistic, better-than-thou and at best highly impersonal. The Scriptures want us *to share* as one family. "I will . . . gather them from all sides . . . and never again shall they be divided."

What we are asked to share, moreover, is the best. That which we prize most, consists not only in art works or mechanical devices or family heirlooms; it especially includes our home, our family, our hours of relaxation and joy, even our family tragedies where we rally around with comforting strength, forgiveness and love. The prophet Ezekiel, always practical minded about details, also adds the injunction that we be united in politics (one prince), in worship (one sanctuary), in neighborhood (one land).

Jesus *lived out* the hopes and the injunctions of Ezekiel. Jesus interacted with politics, religion and social customs. He cured the sick and the handicapped on the Sabbath and broke religious taboos; he threatened political structures where even the high priest was the tool and appointee of the Romans; he ate and drank with publicans and other non-observant people. Jesus was showing how to share the best. His last great miracle was to restore the family of Mary and Martha by raising their brother Lazarus from the dead. Many people were assembling at their home in Bethany and were putting their faith in Jesus.

We have suffered greatly in our effort to restore peace and to share freely within our family, relation and neighborhood. We have felt the pain of the post Vatican II Church, wherein many cherished customs were seemingly lost in the name of renewal and reunion. As the Church struggles through this difficult period, we seek to recover the truly good things, momentarily lost, only that they be shared and thereby transformed.

To realize the prophecy of Ezekiel and to fulfill his own commandment from the heavenly Father, Jesus seemed to lose everything. He was killed! Yet, because he lost his life in an act of sharing the best, that life was raised up to new glory.

> He who scattered Israel, now gathers
> them together,

He guards them as a shepherd his flock.
I will turn their mourning into joy,
I will console and gladden them after
their sorrow.

HOLY WEEK

Monday of Holy Week

Is 42:1-7. Song of the Suffering Servant. Victory is achieved quietly, yet it extends to all the earth.

John 12:1-11. At the house of Lazarus Mary anointed Jesus' feet. Jesus explained: ". . . they prepare me for burial."

The Scripture readings combine a gentle personal devotion towards Jesus, manifested in Mary's silent anointing of Jesus' feet, with an apostolic concern for world salvation, announced by the Lord's servant as "a light to the nations." The two ideas slip together like hand into glove. No language is as universal and persuasive as gentleness.

Yet we ponder these words at the beginning of a week disrupted by violence and execution! Today we read of the crowds streaming to Bethany in order to see the empty tomb and the living body of Lazarus; at the end they will be filling another tomb with the mangled body of Jesus. A week of such violent contrasts would normally erupt in words of hate and revenge; instead, love, forgiveness and hope dominate the prayers and readings.

The account of Mary's anointing the feet of Jesus is well chosen for the Monday of Holy Week; Jesus sees her action as a preparation for his own burial. Mary, however, saw it as a supreme moment of loving devotion towards Jesus. Such should be our attitude this week. Our entire attention should be directed towards Jesus himself; every other distraction should be removed or avoided. Someone we love dearly is approaching death. We must be silently at his side, to show compassion and concern, as often and as long as possible.

At times such as this we communicate the most in silence, because words say very little. Thoughts are so profound that they can only be intuited. What is desired most is our loving presence.

Isaiah has caught the sombre, hopeful, strong silence of this week. The passage in chapter 42, the first Song of the Suffering Servant, was composed towards the end of a prophetic career marked at first by exuberant hope and wondrous consolation (see chapters 40-41 in the book of Isaiah), ending with obstruction and rejection (45:9-13). The prophet's response leaped beyond the narrow confines of his earlier apostolate. "It is too little," he had to admit, to be the Lord's servant solely to restore the survivors of Israel. He hears the divine commission: "I made you a light to the nations!" (Is 49:6; 42:6).

The attitude of comfort and gentleness remains, as the Lord's spirit rests upon this beloved servant. These words of Isaiah were quoted at Jesus' baptism when he began his public ministry (Luke 3:22). They are now repeated again as he advances toward a new, worldwide apostolate through the door of his death.

The way by which Jesus is to bring "justice on the earth" is totally different from the triumphant, prestigious, military might of Cyrus the Great, the Persian monarch then on the march towards a world empire. Jesus' way, unfortunately, may also contrast with our ways of dealing with others, even in our own family, community or neighborhood.

> Not crying out, nor shouting
>> not making his voice heard in the street.

A bruised reed he shall not break,
>
> and a smoldering wick he shall not
> quench.

"Not crying, nor shouting"—as others cry out against him, even for his death, even, indeed, against a woman who anoints his feet. Jesus will not permit this smoldering wick—the kindly act of this lonely but timid woman—to be quenched. How courageous she was, to enter a room where such criticism could rebound against her! How gentle of Jesus to defend her and all the poor of the world. How courageously Jesus is approaching his own violent death, which he undergoes so gently. Thus he opens the eyes of the blind—our eyes—to this universal language of salvation.

The Lord is my light and my salvation;
>
> whom should I fear?
The Lord is my life's refuge;
>
> of whom should I be afraid?

Tuesday of Holy Week
Is 49:1-6. Second Song in which the Suffering Servant struggles with frustration yet recognizes a divine summons to be "a light to the nations."
John 13:21-33, 36-38. Jesus announces his betrayal by Judas and by Peter. In between he declared: "Now is the Son of Man glorified, and God is glorified in him."

For the Suffering Servant as well as for Jesus, disappointment and even betrayal led to their own glorification and to the accomplishment of their God given vocation. Life cannot and should not be planned that way. To presume that friends will betray us would be destructive of our own character and of all our best relationships. A couple is never advised to enter marriage with the assumption that infidelity will take place!

Yet, setbacks, defeats and frustration happen. People disappoint us. Our best plans go up in smoke. Small disillusionments catch up with us when a purchase does not adequately live up to the advertisement or when a long awaited vacation is snarled in bad weather. Much bigger disappointments scar our memory when our fervent hopes for family or community or for our own individual lives fade and droop. We would never recognize how pale and dull are the landscapes of our lives if we had not entertained exceptional possibilities and wonderful hopes. We feel victimized by our goodness and optimism.

The prophet recognized this good and holy source of his life. He wrote: "The Lord called me from birth [this way], from my mother's womb he gave me my name." In a biblical context name always carried a vocational call and divine sense of destiny. The servant felt like "a sharp-edged sword"; he was able to think clearly and perceive keen possibilities. Yet, he was concealed in the shadow of the Lord's arm, a polished arrow in the Lord's quiver. His hopes died aborning. He was led to await wonderful results, but, instead,

. . . I had toiled in vain,
and for nothing, uselessly spent my strength.

At this moment the servant could have given up and stopped believing in God! Or the servant could have decided how useless to wait any longer, and quit! Or again the servant might have felt the futility of continuing in a dead cause, and pulled out!

Instead of dying with bitter frustrations both the servant as well as Jesus realized that they were called into earthly life, not for an earthly ambition, but to achieve a delicate love and a faithful consecration with God and with their neighbors within the scope of their earthly life. Although we do not and should not plan on frustration or infidelity, as already mentioned, nonetheless such sad episodes can turn our mind and heart to the Lord's glory and to our friendship with the Lord, more effectively than any other means.

If our disappointments spring from our wonderful God-given hopes, then we must frequently return to the Lord to appreciate the purpose of these hopes. Such renewal is necessary. We will all admit how easily we are distracted from the Lord by the busy preoccupations of our work.

These frustrations then turn out to be very liberating. We are freed from a workaholic existence to an ever more "person" oriented life. The first person in our lives must be God. Such was Jesus' response. In between announcements of the two betrayals, one by Judas and the other by Peter, Jesus declared:

Now is the Son of Man glorified
and God is glorified in him.

The Servant wrote exquisitely:

Yet my reward is with the Lord,
my recompense is with my God.

Through this very intense, very interior bond with God the Father the Servant and Jesus live even through death for a new and more stupendous call reaching

beyond all their earlier hopes. Seen and accepted this
way, trials which cut across and demolish our first
hopes lead us to a new and more profound relationship
of prayer and trust with God, and in this way trials
liberate us from small restrictive hopes that God may
lead us to a "salvation . . . to the ends of the earth."

> You are my hope, O Lord;
>> my trust, O God, from my youth.
> On you I depend from birth;
>> from my mother's womb you are my
>> strength.

Wednesday of Holy Week
Is 50:4-9. The third Song of the Suffering Servant details
    personal suffering and public humiliation but at no
    loss of peace, confidence and dignity.
Matt 26:14-25. Woe to that person by whom the Son of
    Man is betrayed.

Betrayal is one of the worst crimes to commit or to
experience; it may even be the most destructive of all. It
wrenches us apart at the core of our existence, where
we establish and maintain our essential relationships of
trust, love and security. Every sin injures the confidence and faith which we should grant and receive, in
order to carry on the normal business and routine of
life; every evil act makes us a bit more fearful of others
and raises barriers between us. Betrayal, however, cuts
the deepest of all and inflicts the worst scars upon our
psyche. This type of injury usually incapacitates us for
good, happy living; we tend to isolate ourselves. Bitter
in loneliness, the betrayed person is unable to set up the

normal contacts prerequisite for even a simple conversation.

For the very reason that betrayal strikes most profoundly at the heart of our existence, it opens up the deepest levels of our love and reflection. It offers an opportunity to dedicate our *whole* selves *anew* to God. It enables us to purify our motives in our relationships. It raises such crucial questions: do I love others only that they may love me? It asks me to *forgive as I am forgiven by God.* It seeks its confidence, not in flesh and blood, but in God. It finds its true dignity not in public recognition but in its conscience pure and sincere before God.

Even though Jesus knew that Judas was seeking an opportunity to betray him, Jesus invited him with the other apostles to recline and dine with him. Jesus made a final stab at preventing this betrayal by questioning Judas and forcing him to admit his heinous deed. Maybe if Judas says it as it is, he will be repelled by such an ugly act. If Jesus made every attempt to win Peter back to repentance after thrice denying him, then Jesus must have tried desperately to retrieve Judas.

Through it all Jesus still speaks of "my appointed time." He did not lose confidence in his heavenly Father, nor did he cut human contacts. Jesus renewed his profound consecration to God's Holy Will; he believed that this Father was decidedly leading the life of his son to its proper fulfillment.

The Suffering Servant of Isaiah demonstrates exceptional strength acquired through a docile attitude of listening morning after morning. The tongue which speaks has been well-trained. The servant suffered severe humiliations: his beard plucked, his face slapped and spit upon. Yet, as he stared ahead through the tears dropping from his eyes and mingling with the spit cast upon his cheeks, he declared: "I am not disgraced." It is unbelievable how the Servant could maintain any honor at all. At such degradation most people go to pieces, lose all their inhibitions and commit the strangest, careless crimes, but not the Servant!

The Servant remained strong and involved. He was anxious to refer the whole matter to a law court. The Hebrew language abounds with technical, legal terms: for instance, "upholds my right" translates the Hebrew word for "vindicator"; "wishes to oppose me" equals "impeachment"; "appear together" means "take the witness stand," *etc*. The Servant was not broken in spirit, but surrendered in spirit totally to God: "See, the Lord God is my help; who will prove me wrong?"

Jesus turned frequently to the four Songs of the Suffering Servant in the Prophecy of Isaiah, in order to absorb strength, dedication and new peace. Jesus has given us an example. Nothing outside of us can ever rob us of our interior peace and dignity, unless we let it do so! In fact, our God-given goodness will be all the more evident in our silent strength and serene love. Yet, like Jesus we need to turn daily to the Scriptures for light, encouragement, and the example of other saintly men and women.

> See, you lowly ones, and be glad;
> > You who seek God, may your hearts
> > be merry!
> For the Lord hears the poor,
> > and his own who are in bonds he
> > spurns not.

Thursday of Holy Week (Evening Mass)
Ex 12:1-8, 11-14. Old Testament ritual of the Paschal

Supper, including the application of blood upon each home. Commemoration of Israel's liberation from Egyptian slavery.

1 Cor 11:23-26. St. Paul's account of the Last Supper, adding that thereby "you proclaim the death of the Lord until he comes."

John 13:1-15. Jesus washes the feet of the twelve. "What I have done, so you must do."

On this evening when we commemorate Jesus' institution of the Holy Eucharist, our principal biblical passage is taken from the gospel of John. Yet, unlike the other three gospels and despite the long farewell address of Jesus at the Eucharistic table, John does not include any account of the institution of the Eucharist. He almost seems to imply that we do not need the Eucharist in order to possess the "real" presence of Jesus. Jesus himself stated: "where two or three are gathered in my name there am I in their midst" (Matt 18:20).

Other biblical passages come to mind. In John's gospel Jesus says during his final discourse:

> Anyone who loves me will be true to
> my word, and my Father will love him;
> we will come to him
> and make our dwelling place with him.
> (John 14:23)

> I am the vine, you are the branches,
> He who lives in me and I in him,
> will produce abundantly. (John 15:5)

St. Paul wrote: "You are the temple of God" (1 Cor 3:16).

The Eucharist, however, bestows upon us a *very*

special kind of presence. It is important enough that the three synoptic gospels of Matthew, Mark and Luke besides St. Paul in First Corinthians give considerable attention to the institution of the Eucharist. Eucharistic references are scattered throughout all four gospels, especially in the narrative of the multiplication of loaves and fishes. In the Eucharist Jesus is no more really present than in ourselves as his temple or as the vine attached to the branches. Yet, in the Eucharist, *first* Jesus is present without human distraction and sin which accompany his indwelling in us; we can focus attention unreservedly, even mystically upon Jesus alone. *Second*, Jesus is present in the Eucharist with immediate, insistent demands for family love and forgiveness. This family reaches out to include *all* men and women everywhere. We must so love that we are willing and happy to invite *everyone* to our family dinner table. Such is truly the *real* presence of Jesus. The Eucharist lives out the words of Jesus: "where two or three are gathered in my name, there am I in their midst." In the Eucharist we do not pick two or three of our best friends but we eat and drink with *anyone* who approaches the table of the Lord.

Sensitive to our situation and conscious of this severe expectation, Jesus gave us a personal example, of humble forgiveness. He washed and dried the feet of each of his disciples, even Judas' feet. Why? to "show his love . . . to the *end*." Here "end" means even to this supreme example of charity. Jesus also wanted "to give you an example" of forgiveness and humility, thereby renewing life with fresh vitality. As he said to his disciples, "you are entirely cleansed."

To love this much and to forgive this totally, a person must have suffered greatly. Such love does not come easily, neither then and certainly not in our world of racial, ethnic and even family feuds. The cost is great; the suffering is significant. At our Eucharist where such love and forgiveness take place, we "proclaim the death of the Lord until he comes."

The lamb—Jesus—has been slain and its blood applied to the doorposts and lintels of our hearts, of our homes, of our churches. Without Jesus' example of washing feet and dying, we could never have mustered such forgiving love.

This love liberates us out of our "Egypt" of oppression where we were our own victims of hate, fear, jealousy, antagonism! We go forth in haste for a new wonderful life, a full life of love. When such a love becomes totally real and immediately evident, the Eucharist then gives place to heaven. As we await this glorious vision, we proclaim by the Eucharist "the death of the Lord until he comes."

> How shall I make a return to the Lord
> > for all the good he has done for me?
> The cup of salvation I will take up,
> > and I will call upon the name of the
> > Lord.

Good Friday

Is 52:13-53:12. Fourth Song of the Suffering Servant. "Pierced for our offenses . . . by his stripes we were healed. . . . Because of his affliction, he shall see light in fulness of days . . . [and] justify many."

Hebr 4:14-16; 5:7-9. Jesus Christ, a great high priest, tempted in every way that we are, yet without sinning; he offered prayers . . . with tears to be saved

from death, and learned obedience from what he
suffered.

John ch 18-19. The Passion of Our Lord Jesus
Christ.

Today we assembly as a family, sorrowing over the
death of a most beloved member. We are the people
seen in vision by the prophet Zechariah:

> They shall look on him whom they have thrust
> through, and they shall mourn for him as one
> mourns for an only son, and they shall grieve
> over him as one grieves over a first-born.
> (Zech 12:10)

We are not gathered at the death bed but rather at the
wake or funeral home. So conscious are we of Jesus'
death, in all its tragic reality, that we do not celebrate
Mass. We move away from the symbolic or sacramental
commemoration and fix our sorrowing and stunned
gaze upon the broken, dead body of Jesus!

> Many are amazed at him—
> so marred was . . . his appearance
> beyond that of mortals—so shall
> he startle many nations. . . .

As we gather in mourning, the three biblical
readings enable us to ponder the death of Jesus sorrowfully but also peacefully and even ecstatically. The
Bible does not focus so realistically upon the corpse of
Jesus that we should possess a museum record of
Jesus' death with movies, snapshots and cassette re-
cordings. Rather the Bible moves delicately back and

forth between the dead Jesus and the sorrowing community. All three passages were born in the heart of a saint meditating through the Scriptures upon human-divine tragedy. Each draws heavily upon the earlier, pre-existing scriptures and weaves its words into a new expression of sorrow and hope, death and life.

Isaiah in composing the Suffering Servant Songs weaves together not only the phrases and ideas of the prophet Jeremiah, but also the promises entrusted to the Davidic family as well as the remembrance of liturgical sacrifices. In the epistle to the Hebrews the author is filled with the thoughts and theology of Paul and John, but he has also contemplated Jesus' agony in the garden in relation to temple sacrifices and priesthood. John's passion narrative is so heavily liturgical that Jesus is continually seen not only as God (in John the cohort and guards fall to the ground before Jesus, while in the other gospels Jesus falls to the ground in the garden of Gethsemane) but also as the source of Christian liturgy (the blood and water from his side indicate Eucharist and Baptism).

We are asked to do the same. We are inspired to realize very deeply the tragedy of Jesus' death in the context of our own sorrows and trials. We are tempted, so was Jesus, and we can learn obedience from what we suffer. This obedience insures our fidelity to God, to one another, and to the Holy Scriptures. In our own helplessness we are assured the support not only of God and His family, but also of the Bible which articulates the deepest responses of each. It is the Word of God. We are able to sustain greater pain because of this marvelous support. Our finest instincts are resonated in the most beautiful words of all times and shared within a liturgical, praying community.

A liturgical community then imparts strength, dignity and life to moments of death. What could have remained hideous and beyond recall is transformed into beauty, hope and a continuous call to heroic goodness. Death becomes a force for life, physical agony can reflect interior serenity.

Jesus then becomes our "great high priest," sympathizing with us, for he has experienced our weakness and pain, even our temptations. Our sobs are gathered up in his so that his prayer is heard within our peace. Perfected thus in our community of faith, Jesus is "a source of eternal salvation."

> Happy are those who mourn;
> > God will comfort them!
> Happy are those who are humble;
> > they shall receive what God has
> > > promised. (Matt 5:4-5 Good
> > > > News Bible)

PART TWO

Sundays of Lent

"A" CYCLE

First Sunday of Lent—"A" Cycle

Gen 2:7-9; 3:1-7. Despite the beautiful garden where the Lord God made a home for the first couple, they disobeyed and lost their innocence.

Rom 5:12-19. "Just as through one person's disobedience all became sinners, so through one person's obedience all shall become just." (CS)

Matt 4:1-11. Jesus, while fasting in the desert is tempted three times by the devil.

We are not usually tempted by what is obviously bad. Rather, temptations emerge out of goodness which we desire selfishly for ourselves alone. Temptations change at once to invitations to greater goodness, once we recognize the possibility to share properly and happily with others. If we are tempted to anger and violence, the human responses can be turned to upholding one's convictions and to defending energetically the rights of the poor. Temptations to sexual sins can be turned around into a delicate and tender concern for every other person and become the source of a happy, romantic marriage.

Strange as it sounds, goodness provides the occasion for temptation, goodness around about us in other people, places and events, goodness within us in our talents and values. The extraordinary goodness of the garden of paradise, heightened by the exceptional personal gifts within Adam and Eve, erupted into selfish claims, therefore, into temptation and sin. Jesus was tempted while fasting and praying in the desert. Here he was led by the Spirit; here he realized the incomparable gifts which he, a human being, possessed because of his being Son of God with a messianic mission. In the desert the devil suggested: "Because you are so saintly and so powerful work those extravagant miracles quickly, at once, and the messianic triumph all over the world will be accomplished! Why wait?"

Jesus, however, waited and concentrated upon his public ministry. This way of God was long, at times tedious and in the end seemingly a failure. The work had to be handed over to apostles and disciples, and as it continues into our own day, it is still unfinished. Maybe we are tempted to think that Jesus should have followed the devil's advice and carried out the world's salvation as quickly as turning stones into bread. Then all the kingdoms of the world would be his, enthusiastically acclaiming this wonder-worker who can even throw himself from the highest and most conspicuous spot of the temple and remain unharmed.

Jesus waited; for only by a slow process of thought, prayer and dedication can salvation be achieved according to God's holy will. This salvation must be shared with everyone before individual persons can consider themselves fully saved.

The whole human race felt the consequences when Adam and Eve sinned. As our first parents, they acted as responsible agents for all their family. Every member of their family in receiving the gift of life participated in the strengths and weaknesses, the wealth and the problems of their parents.

All of us are again one family in the new and final Adam, Jesus Christ, all of us receive the benefits of his goodness. Both sin and holiness, then, are received from our first parents, Adam and Jesus. These are not external signs or cloaks wrapped around us which can be traded off. Rather sin and holiness are deeply interior responses of life, at the source of life. In Adam we are selfish and tend to misuse goodness; in Jesus we are so strong as to share without losing. To adapt these interior dispositions takes much time, if it is to be done personally, at the core of what determines our personality and entire sense of values.

Time is also required if we are to share with *all* our brothers and sisters. In fact, so intense is this bond of union that all of us are Adam; all of us are Christ. What anyone does affects everyone. No one can be fully saved until the full family membership is complete and all share in the goodness of everyone else.

> A clean heart create for me, O God,
> > and a steadfast spirit renew within me.
>
> Cast me not out from your presence,
> > and your holy spirit take not from me.

Second Sunday of Lent — "A" Cycle

Gen 12:1-4. Abraham is promised to be a great nation and a model of blessings for all other nations if he obediently goes forth "to a land that I will show you."

2 Tim 1:8-10. Not by our own merits but by the grace in Christ Jesus has God saved us. Therefore, we ought to bear our share of the hardships which the gospel entails.

Matt 17:1-9. Jesus, wondrously transfigured, is joined by Moses and Elijah; a voice out of the clouds says: "This is my beloved Son on whom my favor rests. Listen to him."

Jesus, transfigured so that his divinity shone through his human body like sunlight beaming within alabaster, announces the extraordinary possibilities at the depths of everyone of us. As a "temple of God" (1 Cor 3:16) where the Father, Son and Holy Spirit have "come . . .[to] make our dwelling place" (John 14:23), we carry within us "the Holy Spirit . . ., the pledge of our inheritance, the first payment against the full redemption of a people God has made his own, to praise his glory" (Eph 1:13-14). The glory which will transform us when we share in the resurrection of Jesus, already resides at the base or core of our existence. Here Jesus dwells, one with the Father and the Spirit, in this inner Holy of Holies. We already possess what we will be; glory in the remembrance of our future, transfiguring our lives now in small but significant ways.

Heavenly glory, moreover, does not come from outside like a whirlwind to whisk us off the planet earth in a shock of wonder; rather, it is already developing within us like seed planted within mother earth still surrounded with darkness. Occasionally its inspirations and insights, its secret hopes and joys, break through and transfigure, at least momentarily, the surface doldrum of our life. These are those wonderful yet awesome moments when God summons us to leap beyond all earthly limitations and with our earthly body to perform heroic deeds. These moments are fleeting dreams come true.

We all know such moments. We can all testify that our finest actions have flowed from such sudden inspirations. Abraham knew such an hour when God said: "Go forth from the land of your kinsfolk and from your father's house to a land that I will show you." Abraham and his wife were an elderly couple without children, yet God promised to make them a great nation. Believing, they set out and as St. Paul adds, they were "hoping against hope" (Rom 4:18). World salvation lay within their bodies and yet as Paul wrote again in the same passage, their bodies were "as good as dead . . . yet, he never questioned or doubted God's promise" (Rom 4:19-20). Their obedience to an extraordinary, interior inspiration transfigured their lives with hope.

These moments of dreams and visions can frighten us, so great is the joy of expectation, so fearful its cost, so undetermined its way of fulfillment. We can and should seek advice, yet the ultimate decision must be our own, alone with God.

Counselors can help immensely to point out signs and signals, also from God and evident in our character and past experience. They can judge if we have been willing as Paul wrote to Timothy, to "bear your share of the hardships which the gospel entails." If not, then we need more time for prayer and penance, self-denial and self-discipline. A good counselor, however, must also count on the extraordinary grace of Jesus, present in each person. Another sign from our past experience lies in the exceptional graces already received and experienced. An unusually good counselor, then, judges not just from human accomplishments but from the hidden motivation from God who "has saved us and called us to a holy life, not because of any merit of ours, but according to his own design—the grace held out to us in Christ Jesus."

As already mentioned, we may need more time for prayer and penance. Lent is such a period of time when we purify our desires of false selfish concerns, when we deepen our awareness of Jesus' indwelling presence.

Lent is our journey up the mount of Transfiguration.

> Our soul waits for the Lord,
> > who is our help and our shield.
> May your kindness, O Lord, be upon us
> > who have put our hope in you.

Third Sunday of Lent — "A" Cycle

Ex 17:3-7. When the Israelites grumbled about their
difficult times in the desert the Lord instructed
Moses to strike a rock that water flow from it for the
people to drink.

Rom 5:1-2, 5-8. While we were still sinners, Christ died
for us. This hope will not disappoint us.

John 4:5-42. Jesus converses with the Samaritan
woman at the well, declaring that people will worship
the Father neither at Jerusalem nor at Mt. Gerizim,
but "in Spirit and truth."

The Bible frequently introduces the universal
symbol of water. Water means life; without it the land
hardens into a desert wilderness (Gen 2:5; Deut 8:7).
Water cleanses and refreshes (Num 8:7; Is 41:17-20).
Water can mount a mighty power and sweep with the
devastating force of a storm, a flood or a tidal wave (Gen
7-9; Mark 4:35-41). These and other properties of water
are reflected in Israel's liturgy and in prophetic preaching. The prophets tended to interiorize the symbolism
of water (Jer 2:12-18; Ez 36:25). Jesus returned to the
persistent presence of water to instill faith in God's
continuous love: "Your heavenly Father . . . rains on
the just and the unjust" (Matt 5:45). He concluded that
we are to do more than simply love those who love us.

This same merciful care of God is manifest in today's readings. The people are grumbling against Moses as if he brought them out into the desert to kill them, their children and their livestock of thirst. God nonetheless works a miracle to provide water. The Samaritan woman tended to be sarcastic in speaking with Jesus, a Jew. The incident in the Book of Exodus is reversed. The people possess a bountiful supply of water and this time God has good reason to complain against their immorality. Yet, God, in Jesus, asks from one of his sinful creatures: "Give me a drink."

With extraordinary patience does God listen and respond to his human family. Whether he is faced with ill-humored complaints or insolent sarcasm, God is willing to sit down and talk. In John's gospel we are amazed how Jesus gradually thaws out the coldness of the woman and slowly removes her defenses. She is led from a haughty: "Who are you, Jew?" to a selfish realism: "Give me some that I won't have to come here so often!" to a personal curiosity: "I have no husband—but why do you say that?" to an act of faith: "You are a prophet."

Other series of conversations between Jesus and his disciples or among the townspeople follow this same route—from surprise or sarcasm to interior belief. Jesus, we see, gave people time and space! He first listened before he spoke or asked a further question. He accepted people where they were and treated them with serious concern. If he asked a small editorial question it was only that *they* would be able to come up with the leading, essential question.

St. Paul meditates aloud on this divine pattern. Even if "it is rare that anyone should lay down his life for a just man, . . . barely possible. It is precisely in this that God proves his love for us; that while we were still sinners, Christ died for us." This love, Paul also points out, "has been poured out in our hearts through the Holy Spirit who has been given to us." Such overwhelming consideration on Jesus' part to sit down by the well and talk with us sinners, even to the extent of giving up his life for us, sweeps through us like blood in our arteries and veins and makes our whole life something different.

We are obliged to imitate Jesus. If God had forgiven us simply by signing a legal document of amnesty, yet otherwise left us to remain the same kind of person as before, we might be expected to continue in our old habits. When, however, God's love reaches the core of our existence and transforms us from within, then we must follow Jesus' example. Otherwise we destroy ourselves!

Lent asks us to meditate on God's humble, considerate way of interacting with us and to pray for the strength to respond to others with the same listening ear, gentle heart, patient forbearance. How badly these qualities are needed. Jesus said to his disciples when they returned to the well: "Open your eyes and see! The fields are shining for harvest . . . One person sows, another reaps." All about us God has sown goodness in people's hearts. At first we may encounter only their grumbling. But if we listen patiently, we will harvest much goodness.

> Oh that today you would hear his voice:
> > Harden not your hearts as at Meribah,
> > as in the day of Massah in the desert,
> Where your fathers tempted me;
> > they tested me though they had seen my works.

Fourth Sunday of Lent — "A" Cycle

1 Sam 16:1, 6-7, 10-13. God judges not by external
    appearances but by what he sees in the heart. David,
    young, spontaneous and innocent is preferred to his
    older and stronger brothers. After his anointing the
    Spirit of the Lord rushed upon him.
Eph 5:8-14. Live as children of "light [which] produces
    every kind of goodness and justice and truth."
John 9:1-41. On the Sabbath Jesus mixed spittle with
    dirt, and with the mud he restored sight to a man blind
    from birth. This man was later rejected from the
    synagogue for confessing Jesus as Messiah.

While last Sunday's Bible readings focused on the
symbolism of water, today's offer a prophetic challenge
drawn from the symbolism of light. In an opening conversation prompted by the sight of a blind man, Jesus
directed attention at once to the "night . . . when no one
can work" and to himself as "the light of the world." To
appreciate his statement we need to recall the role of
light in our daily existence.

The light which emanates from the sun or is produced by electricity actually puts nothing new into our
lives. It simply makes it possible to see whatever is
there and thus to achieve good relationships and know
what to do. If we walk into a room without light, we are
liable to crash into tables and chairs. With light spread
across the same space, all of its furniture and decora-
tions are appreciated at once and we reach a good
relationship with them, sitting at the chairs, reading or
eating at the table. If we walk outdoors and meet the
warm sunlight we can almost see the grass grow and the
flowers burst into bloom. Sunlight does not plant the
grass or flowers but through its life-caressing warmth it
develops the full potential of life within mother earth.

Jesus stated, "I am the light of the world." Very humbly Jesus claimed no special power to create or radically change; instead he makes it possible for eyes encased in darkness to see once again what was already in existence. What cures the blind man is not simply the power to distinguish tables and chairs or to behold people and the landscape of their lives; rather, the blind man really sees when he confesses Jesus as the Messiah and center of all human existence. The blind man now miraculously cured can perceive an entirely new hope and purpose in life.

Life is more than squabbling over small details like the question: did somebody mix saliva with dirt and apply the mud to a person's eyes *and so* break the Sabbath? When faced with this jealous and pompous legalism, the man born blind quickly dismissed the facetious question and remarked very simply: "I know not whether he [Jesus] is a sinner or not . . . I know this much: I was blind before; now I can see." As the questions drone, at times with understated scorn, the man who can see replied plainly and innocently: "If this man [Jesus] were not from God, he could never have done such a thing."

The legalistic, better-than-thou opponents of the man once blind but cured by Jesus "threw him out bodily". Darkness closed in on them. They are really the blind ones! They live in darkness, blinded to the normal expressions of goodness, unable to rejoice that a man born blind can now see. Their set of values and their sense of personal relationships are shrouded in selfish darkness. Obsessed with their own interests they cannot see God's world. Where there should be rejoicing and dancing, they crash into the chairs and tables and throw the man out bodily!

"It is shameful," St. Paul wrote, "even to mention

the things these people do." How is it possible to forget that a blind man can see and then to argue over mud? Did Jesus deliberately use mud—the question comes to mind—just to show how muddled up these false teachers are in their tiny dark world?

Jesus brings us back to the real world in its freshness, goodness, and wholesomeness. Light not only enables us to see but pure light makes sure that we see the world and people as they really are. We are reminded of the various sons of Jesse summoned before Samuel in the first reading and yet not chosen by God. "Do not judge from appearance or looks or from . . . lofty stature, because . . . the Lord with strong light looks into the heart." David, the youngest son, uncontaminated by false values and selfish ambitions, fresh from "tending the sheep," unspoiled and open to the Lord's will, is the Lord's choice.

During Lent we fast and give alms, we pray and wait, so that the Lord will purify our eyes and straighten out our values. Humbled into the spontaneity of David and the common sense of the man cured of blindness, we now put everything together rightly—in Jesus, "the light of the world."

> The Lord is my shepherd.
> He guides me in right paths
>   for his name's sake.
> Even though I walk in the dark valley
>   I fear no evil; for you are at my side
> with your rod and your staff
>   that give me courage.

Fifth Sunday of Lent—"A" Cycle
Ez 37:12-14. God will raise his people from the grave,

place his spirit within them, and settle them upon their land.

Rom 8:8-11. The Spirit which raised Jesus from the dead dwells in us and will bring our mortal bodies to new life.

John 11:1-45. For God's glory and for the sake of greater faith among his disciples, Jesus calls Lazarus back to life.

Although Lazarus returns from death to life, still attention focuses principally on Jesus and our relationship with Jesus today. Jesus summed it up so very well in his response to Martha:

> *I am the Resurrection and the Life:*
> Whoever believes *in me*,
>> though he should die, will come to life;
> And whoever is alive and believes *in me*
>> will never die.

Resurrection then is not so much a theological problem as it is a religious experience. It is not an extravagant miracle happening out there; it means the transforming presence of Jesus within us. The resurrection is not completed when our dead bodies are raised to life but instead when the spirit of Jesus dwells within us, yet, not simply within each of us individually but within all of us as one family.

Jesus *did* raise Lazarus back to life; Jesus himself was to rise from the tomb. St. Paul wrote: "If Christ has not been raised [from the dead], our preaching is void of content and your faith is empty too" (1 Cor 15:14). The Christian religion, however, does not consist in the theological discussions on the nature and reality of the resurrection, but on the person of Jesus alive right now in our very midst and ready to change our lives at this moment.

In today's biblical readings St. Paul centers discussion where it ought to be: "The Spirit of God who raised Jesus from the dead dwells in you." Even if our bodies seem dead, our own spirit lives because of justice. The Spirit stirs up serious tensions and wonderful joys. The Spirit can impel us to exceptional deeds of "love, joy, peace, patient endurance, kindness, generosity, faith, mildness and chastity" (Gal 5:22-23). These "fruits of the spirit" are demanding. At times, again writes St. Paul, it is necessary to crucify "the flesh with its passions and desires" (Gal 5:24). Yet, even in what seems to be death, we experience an intense inner power which we know to be the Spirit, raising us up to new life even at the same time that we are dying.

Our devotion to Jesus may appear over-demanding. It may even seem to have destroyed the possibilities of power, wealth, prestige and satisfaction in our lives. All this may seem like the dead body of Lazarus in the tomb. The opportunities of the good life are finished. Perhaps, before the "end" came, we prayed to Jesus—like Mary and Martha—to come to our rescue and save us. We begged Jesus not to let this moment or last chance to pass us by, but Jesus did not hear. He deliberately allowed the collapse. Maybe by his stern moral demands he forced the issue and caused the end of our hopes.

Despite such tragic disappointment, Martha and Mary still went out to meet Jesus and said: "Lord, if you had been here, my brother would never have died." As they rebuke Jesus, *they still believed* in his power to transform their lives. They were convinced of Jesus' love; he wept with them over the departure of Lazarus from this life. When Jesus ordered the stone to be rolled back from the cave where Lazarus was buried, his request was first interpreted as a desire to see the face of Lazarus one last time. Martha replied: "[it is too late;] it has been four days now." Jesus insisted that "you would see the glory of God."

Then comes that extraordinary sentence, almost as incredible as Lazarus' resurrection: *"They took away the stone!"* Are we just as strong spiritually to believe and to roll away the stone before *our own* disappointments, failures, frustrations, losses? Do we believe that Jesus weeps with us and orders us to plunge ahead into life? Are we convinced that new life will come out of our profound collapses?

If our spirit is that strong, then we will face every new decision and moment of life with the power of Jesus within us. Tensions and struggles may *seem* to break our mortal endurance, but we will be overwhelmed by the Spirit and sense a thorough communion with Jesus. We will hear those words: "I am the resurrection and the life."

If we die in the service of our neighbor, this new strength will be shared with our neighbor. The prophet Ezekiel, in chapter 37, clearly enunciates the need of "*one* nation upon the land." What actually destroyed us in our former hopes may have been our false, selfish narrow-mindedness. We are alive in our fidelity to the Church, our family, our community.

Out of the depths I cry to you, O Lord;
Lord, hear my voice.

Passion or Palm Sunday: Sixth Sunday of Lent—"A" Cycle

Matt 21:1-11. (Gospel for the Procession) This account of Palm Sunday emphasizes the divinity of Jesus, the fulfillment of prophecy, the messianic acclamation: "he who comes."

Is 50:4-7. Within this prophecy of Isaiah, the third song of the Suffering Servant quietly establishes the strength and dignity of a disgraced but righteous person.

Phil 2:5-11. Jesus emptied himself of his divine dignity to be incarnated in our midst and suffer the humiliation of the cross as a way to glory.

Matt 26:14-27:66. The Passion according to Matthew more than Mark's or Luke's gospel, dramatizes the narrative, i.e., by ending with an earthquake, by providing more details from popular tradition, as the anecdote about Judas and Pilate's wife and by meeting catechetical needs through biblical citations.

In the epistle to the Philippians St. Paul incorporates an early church hymn which quickly follows the full cycle of Jesus' life, eternally with the Godhead, incarnationally as "servant" or "slave" even to the extent of an humiliating and most painful death followed by his exaltation as Lord and God forever. Even in an ordinary English translation, this Christian hymn magnificently surrounds each moment of Jesus' existence with awe and wonder, sorrow and compassion. This response of astonishment and overwhelming grief rings out particularly in the Latin chant, sung repeatedly during the ancient liturgy of Holy Week.

What should be the depth and extent of this, our response to Jesus' death and glorification, is pointed out in the opening phrase: "Your attitude must be Christ's." The Greek words quoted by St. Paul can have a double meaning: either christians must feel towards one another as Christ does, *or* they must have that feeling which springs from their mutual, intimate union in Christ Jesus. In any case the deepest points of our thoughts and compassion should be swept along almost ecstatically, so freely that we are no longer conscious of the effort, as Jesus lived, always obedient to the Father from eternity, on earth and again through death to eternity. This cycle of Jesus' life seemed to plunge him into even greater depths of humiliation and shame. Yet, Jesus maintained an extraordinary composure, strength and peace during the most excruciating pain.

This contrast of shame and dignity strikes us all the more forcefully in the first reading from the Suffering Servant Song. The text seems to contradict itself. Even though the Servant's face was the target of spit and blows and plucking of beard, nonetheless he states very distinctly: "I am not disgraced . . . I shall not be put to shame." This inner strength, like Jesus' at a later age, flowed from a spontaneous spirit of obedience to the promptings of the Spirit. In the first Song of the Suffering Servant, God said: "I have put my spirit upon him" (Is 42:11). Therefore, before he even spoke, he listened "morning after morning." This conviction of having followed the urgings of the Spirit produced a tranquility and dignity, even a "face like flint" to encounter all opposition and remain faithful.

This attitude is not to be confused with stubbornness nor with prejudice. Like Jesus, the Servant granted to others what he hoped to receive from them: encouragement, forgiveness, patience, endurance. To be firmly rooted in God, then, at once means a staunch relationship with *all* God's family. The ecstatic prayer and spontaneous obedience of the Servant at once reached outward with open arms. Such likewise was the spirit of Jesus who became one with all of us where we are all equal, in the helplessness of death. As mentioned earlier, the early Christian hymn in Philippians asked that we feel towards one another as people should, intimately united with Jesus. In the depth of this spiritual bond we obey the needs and hopes of one another.

To respond this humbly and trustfully we must turn repeatedly to Jesus in his Passion, Death and Resurrection. St. Matthew's gospel is particularly helpful. While it reflects liturgical celebration in its order, balance, and grandeur, it also introduces popular stories about the dream of Pilate's wife as well as instructional material from the Old Testament. Most of all the large amount of factual data in itself proves that Jesus really died. Nonetheless, we can hardly believe that it took place. Not even the Old Testament prepares us adequately for the baffling mystery of Jesus' life and death. Only by turning repeatedly to Jesus and to the gospel account of Jesus' death, will we be prepared for what God will ask of us.

> All you who see me scoff at me;
>> they mock me with parted lips,
>>> they wag their heads;
> "He relied on the Lord; let him deliver him,
>> let him rescue him, if he loves him."

"B" CYCLE

First Sunday of Lent — "B" Cycle

Gen 9:8-15. To Noah and his sons and descendants God establishes an everlasting covenant of peace, symbolized by the rainbow.

1 Pet 3:18-22. Just as Noah and his sons and their wives were saved by the ark, we are saved by Baptism; each is a means by which the power of Jesus' resurrection reaches us.

Mark 1:12-15. Jesus is led by the Spirit into the desert, where he is tempted by Satan, surrounded by wild beasts, consoled by angels. Afterwards in Galilee he announces: "The reign of God is at hand!"

The Bible readings astound us by their way of sweeping quickly through every moment of human existence, by explaining one mystery by an opposite mystery, by ending to start all over again. Our mind boggles with the jet speed of movement and the complexities of ideas. For instance, in the temptation scene Jesus seems to return to the first paradise, where our first parents dwelt with wild beasts, angels and devils, were themselves tempted, overcome by sin and condemned to die, only to begin the long process towards world redemption. Jesus, too, is surrounded with beasts and angels, tempted but *not* vanquished by the devil, thereby restores the innocence of the first paradise, and then begins the long process of his missionary career which leads to his death and resurrection.

The first letter of Peter adds more baffling details, stating that Jesus *between* his death and resurrection preached to the spirits of those who had disobeyed in

Noah's days, were destroyed by the flood and confined to prison. Finally, the first reading announces a covenant of everlasting peace upon earth, symbolized by the rainbow. Yet, *First Peter* declares in another passage that "the consummation of all is close at hand" (4:7).

These mysterious Bible readings fit well with the spirit of Lent, when we are called upon to fast and give alms more generously, to pray and read the Holy Scriptures more intensely than is normally our custom. Lent forcefully reminds us that life is much more than eating and sleeping, working and relaxing, handling the everyday duties of our home, neighborhood and occupation. We live always surrounded by angels and devils and the spirits of all the departed. We are placed in between first paradise and our final destination. We have the assurance of God's continual care within the Church to which family we were united by Baptism; we remember the fearful warning that all this can end abruptly by our own death or by the final consummation.

To ignore this world of the spirit and pretend that it doesn't exist is no solution. The spirit world will catch us like a forest fire which is never extinguished simply by willing it to go out. Yet, to accept its existence is to walk into an awesome terrain of mysteries beyond our comprehension and control. We are like Jesus whom "the Spirit sent . . . out towards the desert . . . [a] wasteland [where he was] . . . put to the test by Satan. He was with the wild beasts and angels waited on him." Only by strong continuous prayer, by recalling the presence of Jesus with us can we survive this terrifying yet most consoling experience of the spirit world. If Jesus, as Peter wrote: "died for sins once for all," he can and will "lead you to God." Jesus shares with us his own irreproachable conscience and calls us to God's right hand in heaven where all "angelic rulers and powers are subjected to him."

In Jesus and through Jesus we see the tremendous gap between virtue and vice, goodness and evil. Each takes on overwhelming proportions. The struggle assumes heroic dimensions, out there in the desert wilderness. Yet, in and through Jesus a divine power sweeps into us. We, like Jesus, are "sent by the Spirit." We hear those consoling words, not from angels but from Jesus himself: "The reign of God is at hand! . . . believe in the good news!"

Jesus also says, "reform your ways." These words were spoken in between the two phrases in the preceding text. Reformation of life is a compelling necessity, simply because the odds are so mammoth; satan and the angels are on either side of us. Lent brings us to crucial decisions, perhaps between goodness and evil, certainly between a life of much more fervent prayer and generous love and a life of worldliness and selfishness. These decisions can be a matter of life and death. Even such a trivial question as fasting ought to be seen in a context of world hunger and starvation; the probability of more extended prayer and more frequent participation at holy mass and communion should be viewed in a setting of religious or personal persecution in many parts of this world.

Lent then ushers us into a mysterious world. Therefore, we pray in the responsorial psalm:

Your ways, O Lord, make known to me;
• • •
Guide me in your truth and teach me
for you are God my savior.

Second Sunday of Lent—"B" Cycle

Gen 22:1-2, 9, 10-13, 15-18. On the assumption that God wanted the sacrifice of his only son Isaac, Abraham proceeds to the ritual act of child sacrifice. God blesses Abraham for his willingness to go to such extremes out of obedience to the Lord's will and out of faith in the future.

Rom 8:31-34. God did not spare his own son for our sake. Who can bring a charge against us?

Mark 9:2-10. Jesus' transfiguration and the first announcement of his death and resurrection.

The first two readings from Genesis 22 and Romans 8 reach into the depth for the ultimate gift. The narrative of Genesis begins with: "Take your son Isaac, your only one, the one whom you love . . . offer him up as a holocaust!" Each phrase rends an agonizing cry from the heart: "your son . . . your only one, the one whom you love." Each new word reaches more deeply into the heart and wrenches it with another fearful demand. St. Paul writes with less pathos but equal intensity: "Is it possible that he who did not spare his only Son but handed him over for the sake of us all will not grant us all things besides?"

These two gifts were not the generous overflow of abundance, nor even the last "two small copper coins" of the now penniless widow (Mark 12:41-44), but one's own flesh and blood, the only child with whom the parents' entire life and fortune rested. Each gift is wrenched from the grasp of the parent. Abraham, it seems, was misguided into thinking that his God would want no less than the Canaanite gods. Abraham himself would give no less than his Canaanite neighbor—his first born and only son! To interpret this chapter of Genesis in any other way would reduce God to a very cruel tyrant, playing heartless games. Later the narrator told the story with heart-rending spasm, to communicate how horrendous was this Canaanite practice. It was never to be tolerated in Israel (Ex 13:11-15; Jer 7:31).

When God the Father "did not spare his own Son but handed him over for the sake of us all," God certainly did not send an angel, ordering the Romans to execute Jesus. Nor did God directly intervene in any other way to insure Jesus' death. Jesus' death can be traced politically to a combination of many despicable human reactions: jealousy, fear, hatred, bias, weakness, betrayal, bargaining, mob-violence. Ultimately and most realistically Jesus' death was caused by our sins. If *we* had not sinned, Jesus would not have died. St. Paul repeated this ancient creed: "I handed on to you first of all what I myself received, that Christ died for our sins in accordance with the Scriptures" (1 Cor 15:3).

In both cases, therefore, Isaac and Jesus are delivered over to death for what seems to be very unworthy causes: Abraham's ignorance and our violence and sin.

Our own crises of faith erupt when we seem to be the butt of ignorance and the victims of violence. Questions and challenging fists are raised against heaven when God seems so very cruel or despotic, or helpless or unconcerned—at the sudden death of a child, at a foolish loss of home and security, at long, painful and useless sickness. The list never ends. Each of us can add our own details—when we feel betrayed by God.

Reasons are non-existent or they fall flat. There is no explanation. It seems idiotic to still believe in God. Yet, it is more idiotic and still more hopeless to stop believing. There is nowhere else to turn.

We must repeat Jesus' words in the garden of

Gethsemane: "Abba (O Father), you have the power to do all things. Take this cup from me. But let it be as you would have it, not I" (Mark 14:36). We hang with Jesus on the cross and cry out in a loud voice: "My God, my God, why have you forsaken me?" (Gal 2:19; Mark 15:34). We have no other alternative than to hand over our spirit to the Father (Luke 23:46).

When we make this ultimate act of faith, summoned from the most hidden mysterious depths of our person, then like Jesus we are transfigured. The presence of God exudes a joy, peace, strength, tranquility beyond human explanations. We are transformed because from secret depths we have re-consecrated ourselves in a way beyond human comprehension.

Everything comes together for we are at the pith point of all existence in ourselves and in God. In Jesus the transfiguration scene absorbs words and ideas from the Baptism of Jesus, his agony in the garden, the messianic confession of Peter, his death on the cross. We, too, if we share with Jesus the same faithful consecration to the Father's will, will find our own entire life converging. From beginning to end it will be translucent with God's presence. Unbelievably true as it is, ignorance, sin and violence lead to such a transfiguration. What then will goodness not reproduce?

I will walk in the presence of the Lord,
in the land of the living.

Third Sunday of Lent — "B" Cycle
Ex 20:1-17. The ten commandments.
1 Cor 1:22-25. Christ Crucified, the wisdom and power of God.

John 2:13-25. Jesus cleanses the temple, announces its destruction and rebuilding, and applies the whole episode to his own body destroyed because of sin and raised up again.

In today's Bible readings the will of God is ever more deeply planted in our minds and hearts, and at the same time holiness and sin are seen for their wide, sweeping effects upon the entire family of God's people, and then both goodness and evil center upon Jesus.

The ten commandments originated it seems, as very short, negative statements: "Do not kill; do not commit adultery; do not steal. . . ." Psychologically and spiritually the ten commandments reflect a strong simplicity, undistracted by trivialities and red tape, reducing all questions to a matter of life or death, black or white. True, very often we ought to consider the grey area and attend to minor sicknesses. Nonetheless, there are other times, more rare but also more crucial, when we must take a clear, even dramatic stand for righteousness and truth, for Jesus.

The Old Testament prophets—like Hosea chapter 4 and Isaiah chapter 1—put aside all the small talk. Legal niceties and liturgical rubrics become sinful when the poor are starving and defenseless people are oppressed.

> There is no fidelity, no mercy,
>> no knowledge of God in the land.
> False swearing, lying, murder, stealing
>> and adultery! . . .
> Therefore the land mourns,
>> and everything that dwells in
>>> it languishes. (Hos 4:1-3)

For the prophets to have flung this gauntlet upon the conscience of the people, they had to meditate long upon the ten commandments within the lives of the poor and the oppressed.

This interiorization of the decalogue continued, as the commandments were repeatedly taught and explained to the congregations assembled at prayer or sanctuary. The preacher began to assert motivations for keeping the law:

Only one God, for it was I who brought
you up from the place of slavery.

Keep holy the Sabbath day, for the Lord
also rested on the seventh day.

Because of these reasons laws were prescribing more than external conformity. They reached into the heart of the assembly, into its memory of God's rest, to its traditional teaching of only *one* God for all Israel. The ten commandments thereby supported an extensive family; they united the ancestors with the living community; they placed God at the heart of all the people.

In this strong family bond every small request became important. Love responds that way. At every moment of need everyone responded to brother and sister, father and mother. In fact, all the commandments are addressed to adults. Not children but men and women are admonished to honor father and mother. This sense of devotion can seem overdemanding, weakness and foolishness. St. Paul calls it instead the power and the wisdom of God.

Such it was in Christ Crucified. This death of Jesus is announced very early in John's gospel, again in a setting of community worship. Jesus had just cleansed the temple of buying and selling. His wrath burned against such an outrage. Small things, like selling doves, became a matter of life and death. There was no grey area here!

When Jesus spoke of destroying the temple, his disciples remembered afterwards that "he was talking about the temple *of his body*. Only after Jesus had been raised from the dead did his disciples recall that he had said this." On the cross then the anger of God against sin raged within the very body of Jesus. "For our sakes God made him who did not know sin *to be sin*, so that in him we might become the very holiness of God" (2 Cor 5:21).

Here, mysteriously the commandments are so interiorized that all of us are one in Jesus, one in sin and one in holiness. Only by bearing the weight of one another's sin by our own goodness, by rejecting all our evil through the force of all our fidelity, only thus will the temple be cleansed, the temple which is all of us (2 Cor 6:16).

To be this close to one another as Jesus was may be ridiculed as weakness and foolishness; *we believe* that "God's folly is wiser and his weakness more powerful," than any human person's. In Jesus the commandments are life and resurrection for all of us.

> Lord, you have the words of
> everlasting life.

Fourth Sunday of Lent — "B" Cycle
2 Chron 36:14-17, 19-23. The destruction of Jerusalem followed a long series of sins and the people's rejec-

tion of the Lord's messengers. Through Cyrus, king of Persia, the Israelites are freed from their exile and permitted to rebuild the Jerusalem temple.

Eph 2:4-10. Not because of our merit but on account of God's kindness to us in Christ Jesus, we have been raised up as a new creation, to lead a life of good deeds which God has prepared for us in advance.

John 3:14-21. Just as Moses lifted up the bronze serpent, so must Jesus be lifted up that all who believe may have eternal life in him. God sent this Son, not to condemn the world but to save those who believe in him.

During Lent we are inspired to self-denial that our mind be purified of selfishness and our desires of sensuality, so that we can contemplate God's presence in our heart and his will in our daily lives. Paul put it this way in today's second reading: "to lead the life of good deeds which God prepared for us in advance." To perceive God's holy will and to respond promptly mean that spontaneous reactions be pure and unhampered. Not only is penance an invigorating force but meditation upon the Bible also helps to wash our mind of foolish, self-centered preoccupation by feeding new ideas into our bloodstream and by articulating ideals lost within our subconscious. Meditation thus makes the word of God to be incarnate today as the motivating power of a new creation.

The three readings for this "Gaudete" Sunday provide a healthy example of the Bible's meditating upon the Bible. The Second Book of Chronicles quotes Jeremiah and the Book of Kings; John's gospel cites the ancient book of Numbers; the Epistle to the Ephesians may likely be an anthology of Paul's writings, possibly put together by Paul himself.

In citing the early Scriptures the Bible does not impose the inspired writings rigidly upon its own contemporary world. First, it does not necessarily quote word for word. Jeremiah's famous statement about the "seventy years" of exile is adapted to the law of the Sabbath which required land to rest every seven years (Lev 25:4). The exile, therefore, must take its full course of seven years times ten so that the people can have the time adequately to realize what happened. Even Jeremiah did not consider the seventy years an absolutely unchangeable figure, for he twice identified the starting point differently, first in 665 (Jer 25:1, 11) and again in 593 (Jer 28:1; 29:10). We too must rest and realize what God is about in our lives.

Jesus so adapted the image of the bronze serpent that it comes alive in his own person, as he hangs agonizingly upon the cross. But when we see Jesus on the cross, as when the Israelites looked upon the bronze serpent in the desert, *what* is the object of faith? The question is very important because John wrote: ". . . that all who *believe* may have eternal life *in him*." Both the bronze serpent and Jesus Crucified symbolize *sin* (Num 21:4-9; 2 Cor 5:21)! "To believe" means that we see the terrible effects of our evil in Jesus and so accept what must be sin's deadly toll within ourselves. Our own selves cut their shape upon Jesus, yet Jesus' beautiful peace and continual fidelity cure and transform this weakness.

"God so loved the world" as to order his son to live thoroughly within it, even within its weakness and death. Light thus comes into the world. Light allows us to see ourselves, others and our entire world *as it is!* Yet, it exists this way now in Jesus. When our deeds are brought to full light and exposed they are much more quickly and firmly rejected.

At the same time we choose goodness we are choosing Jesus. Now we are able to follow the lead of good deeds "which God prepared for us in advance." Again, however, this beautiful example of Jesus must be *pondered* and then *adapted* to our own times, questions, obligations, hopes and expectations. Such an adaptation occurred in the Book of Chronicles which saw in the Persian King Cyrus the instrument of fulfilling prophecy. We must look to the real world of politics today, study it seriously with biblical ideals in mind, prayerfully seek God's will, courageously follow our best conscience. From this long and deep contemplation will come the further realization that "salvation is yours through faith. This is not your own doing, it is God's gift."

When God has thus "in Christ Jesus raised us up," we must rejoice. This day will be remembered rightly as "Gaudete" or "Rejoice" Sunday.

> Let my tongue be silenced,
>   if I ever forget you.
> By the streams of Babylon
>   we sat and wept when we
>   remembered Zion.

Fifth Sunday of Lent — "B" Cycle
Jer 31:31-34. A new covenant is inscribed upon the heart so that all may know the Lord.
Hebr 5:7-9. Jesus prayed with loud cries and tears and was heard because of his reverence.

John 12:20-33. Because of his troubled soul Jesus prayed. In answer the Father promised to glorify Jesus from the cross where all people will be attracted to him.

Both the passage in Hebr 5:7-9 and another in John 12:27-28 offer us a biblical meditation upon Jesus' agony in the garden. These Bible texts mark a transition from Jesus to ourselves, from Jesus' lonely and abandoned prayer to our own trials and frustrations. This movement is already evident in the gospels. Mark's gospel, closest to the historical event, directs us most forcefully to Jesus who says: "My heart is filled with sorrow to the point of death. Remain here and stay awake" (Mark 14:34). Matthew's gospel records almost identical words (Matt 26:38). Luke, instead, in the opening words of Jesus, draws our attention away from Jesus to ourselves who need help: "Pray that *you* may not be put to the test" (Luke 22:40).

In John's gospel the episode is transposed from the garden of Gethsemane on Holy Thursday evening as in the other three Gospels to the Jerusalem temple on Palm Sunday. Jesus is surrounded not just by his three favorite, though sleeping disciples, but by a large crowd including gentiles. Jesus and the evangelist are conscious of drawing *all* men and women to the cross, once it has been lifted up. As we read John we can best imagine ourselves already in a church setting, beyond the lifetime of Jesus. Even the element of "glory" surrounds the troubled soul of Jesus as the Christian community meditates on his agony in the garden.

The Epistle to the Hebrews considers Jesus already our "great high priest who has passed into the heavens" able "to sympathize with our weakness" for he was "tempted in every way that we are, yet never sinned." This priest offers "prayers and supplications with loud cries and tears to God." He is heard, and by the strength bestowed by God he became obedient unto death. When thus perfected, "he became the source of eternal salvation for all who obey him."

As we ponder the prayer and agony of Jesus within our community of prayer and within the eucharistic liturgy, we are impressed by the humble obedience of Jesus. Gradually his spirit attracts us and his law is inscribed in our heart. We form a community of love and prayer, of forgiveness and support, within the Church and neighborhood. Together as a Church we realize the one shared covenant inscribed on *all* our hearts. Because covenants are not simply between individuals but between groups of people—and such was the case of the "old" or Mosaic covenant—this new one is to be inscribed on all our *hearts*.

In our agony and loneliness we turn to our entire Church, and here our isolation is broken. Forgiveness is felt at once; we pledge to sin no more. It is not even necessary to teach one another. "All, from least to greatest, shall know me, says the Lord." Teaching is unnecessary, because of the law of love on everyone's heart. As each one speaks, the others realize better the depths of divine wisdom within the words.

True devotion, however, must always return to Jesus. Even if theScriptures move away from Jesus and present a community meditation upon the great moments of Jesus' life, still they always situate this contemplation *within* the life and heart of Jesus. The gospels maintain the context of Jesus' life and ministry. St. Paul insists upon Jesus' continued existence within the Church, which is his body (1 Cor 12:12, 27). We, too, have never prayed if we have simply studied our own problems and projected our own hopes, albeit in Jesus' presence and with his example.

Lent calls us back to Jesus, and the last two weeks bring us poignantly and compassionately before Jesus in his agony, death and resurrection. The new covenant upon our hearts, whereby we love God with all our strength, mind and heart (Deut 6:5), brings tears to our eyes and closes out every distraction. We weep "with loud cries and tears" and are drawn to Jesus "lifted up" upon the cross. We are most willing to lose our lives that we may be where Jesus is. In this intense union the world's prince is driven out and we are re-dedicated to our Lord and Savior.

> A clean heart create for me, O God,
> > and a steadfast spirit renew within me.
> Cast me not out from your presence,
> > and your holy spirit take not from me.

Passion or Palm Sunday — Sixth Sunday of Lent — "B" Cycle

Mark 11:1-10. (Gospel for the Procession) Mark's account of Palm Sunday lets the humble, peaceful character of Jesus' messianic presence make its impression; Matthew's narrative, on the contrary, quotes Scripture more abundantly and emphasizes even the divinity of Jesus.

John 12:12-16. (Alternate Gospel for the Procession) John's narrative is the shortest so that our attention is drawn at once to Jesus' royal status as "King of Israel" and to the necessity of his death and resurrection to appreciate the mysteries of his life and ours.

Is 50:4-7. Within the prophecy of Isaiah this third Song of the Suffering Servant quietly establishes the strength and dignity of a disgraced but righteous person.

Phil 2:5-11. Jesus emptied himself of his divine dignity, to be incarnated in our midst and suffer the humiliation of the cross as a way to glory.

Mark Ch 14-15. The Passion according to Mark is closest of all the gospels to the tragic event and maintains most steadily the bleak and lonely setting of Jesus' death. Yet, the theological purpose of the account is seen not only in the biblical citations but also in the climatic confession of the centurion, "clearly . . . the Son of God."

The Gospel according to Mark dominates today's liturgy and introduces us into the most violent contrasts of Jesus' mission on earth. Only by divesting himself totally of his divinity, even to the point of utter loneliness in his prayer at Gethsemane and of absolute abandonment on the cross, does Jesus manifest his divinity and be acclaimed by the Roman centurion: "Clearly this man was the Son of God." *This man* is evidently human, even to the point of crying out "in a loud voice, 'Eloi, Eloi lama sabachthani?' which means, 'My God, my God, why have you forsaken me?' " These last recorded words of Jesus in Mark's gospel are given in Aramaic first; Mark insists that Jesus really shouted them out. *This man* is that human!

Throughout Mark's gospel Jesus continuously appears very human, much more so than he does in the other evangelists. Jesus could be angry and give "a stern warning" even in the midst of his miracles (Mark

1:25, 43). Jesus could be only half awake and half asleep when first aroused during the storm at sea (Mark 4:38). Yet, everyone senses an extraordinary person beneath this human appearance. Jesus must silence the enthusiasm of the people (Mark 1:44). This phenomenon is frequently called the "messianic secret" in Mark's gospel.

The silence is broken by Peter's confession: "You are the Messiah," yet at once Jesus "gave them strict orders not to tell anyone about him" (Mark 8:29 30). Jesus is not the kind of Messiah that people would presume him to be.

Jesus' ministry continues till his messianic entrance into Jerusalem on Palm Sunday. Yet, here the tone is subdued, especially when compared to the other gospels, and the triumphant procession ends abruptly; Jesus enters the temple — as it were alone with only the twelve — looks around, "but since it was already late . . ., he went out to Bethany" (Mark 11:11).

Only after his death amid desolation and mockery does the Roman centurion acclaim him the "Son of God." On the lips of a pagan this phrase must be taken in its obvious meaning: Jesus is divine. It frequently has a different connotation, however, when read in the Hebrew Bible. At this point, Jesus' messianic mission reaches to the entire world. The Jewish Messiah, confessed by Peter, is the divine Savior of all people. "So that at Jesus' name *every* knee must bend . . . and *every* tongue proclaim . . . Jesus Christ is Lord!"

What convinces all men and women of Jesus' divinity are those extraordinary virtues of patience, forbearance, peace, strength, interior dignity, total self-giving, to possess everything. The Suffering Servant of Isaiah prepared for this messianic role of Jesus. Even though the Servant was shamed by people spitting on his face and pulling on his beard, he still declared: "I am not disgraced . . . knowing that I shall not be put to shame."

Jesus' divinity in Mark's gospel is ultimately established, not by his miracles but by his humanity in its total weakness. Then it became evident in a way understandable to all sincere men and women that Jesus was sustained by a power beyond human control, that this power was so rooted in the depths of himself that it must *be* Jesus. If it *is* Jesus, then it is not just a power but a divine person. "Clearly this man is the Son of God."

> But you, O Lord, be not far from me;
>   O my help, hasten to aid me.
> You, who fear the Lord, praise him.

"C" CYCLE

First Sunday of Lent — "C" Cycle

Deut 26:4-10. At a harvest festival the people offer first fruits and confess a creed enumerating the great moments of Israel's salvation.

Rom 10:8-13. This Baptismal formula confesses that Jesus is Lord, raised from the dead. Everyone who calls upon the name of the Lord will be saved.

Luke 4:1-13. The temptation of Jesus in the desert according to Luke's gospel.

The first two readings raise our hopes to a great letdown. According to Deuteronomy God gave to Israel the "land flowing with milk and honey" after bringing the people out of Egypt with his "strong hand and outstretched arm, with terrifying power, with signs and wonders." Joyfully they make a return of the "first fruits of the product of the soil." Life, with all its signs and wonders, seems so simple, in fact, so *wonderfully* simple!

St. Paul, in the second reading from Romans, reinforces this direct response of divine salvation. Quoting from his favorite Old Testament book of Isaiah, Paul spoke for God in telling the Romans: "No one who believes in me shall be put to shame" for the Lord is "rich in mercy toward all who call upon him."

We know that life is much more complicated in its ways and far less miraculous in its results than these Bible selections indicate. Jesus would agree with us, even reassuring us by his own temptations that he knows the impatience and impulsiveness, the anxieties and false escapes of life. In "the desert for forty days . . . he was tempted by the devil."

Jesus' temptations here at the beginning of his missionary career take a very different form from that at the end in the garden of Gethsemane. On Holy Thursday he was "filled with fear and distress . . . with sorrow to the point of death" and prayed for deliverance from his torturous last hours. In the desert, however, life was just opening up before him. In fact, the temptations are carefully linked in Luke's gospel with the sacred anointing of his Baptism. "The Holy Spirit descended on him in visible form like a dove" after his Baptism (Luke 3:22) and now "Jesus, full of the Holy Spirit, . . . was conducted by the [same] Spirit into the desert where [all that while] he was tempted by the devil."

Jesus was conscious that now the Scriptures were being fulfilled and the year of favor was at hand (Luke 4:19, 21). The power of miracles pulsed within himself; the divine sonship lost by the first Adam, can now be restored to all men and women through his own ministry. The devil tempted Jesus to do it quickly! Why wait?

In Luke's account of the temptation, the third and climatic one is placed at the Jerusalem temple. From the parapet of the temple where the Kidron valley lies far below, the devil says: "Jump!" It would be a magnificent spectacle, with angels hovering about, supporting Jesus, and all the temple crowd bowing in worship!

Certainly it was the Father's will that Jesus complete his messianic work at Jerusalem—Luke is very conscious of this fact—but only from the cross can Jesus say: "It is finished" (John 19:30). Here, in death as he quietly and prayerfully surrendered his spirit to the Father, Jesus would lay the foundation of a new Jerusalem temple. Jesus, therefore, must resist the temptation of a quick messianic victory; he will proceed with the slow process of his preaching and instructing, of his miracles to cure the sick rather than to turn attention to himself, of his praying and offering an example of humble compassion.

We, too, are tempted by our talents. Where we feel capable, we want quick success. We ambitiously seek to dominate others where we have the ability and opportunity to do so. We talk ourselves into thinking that our mastery over others is really for their benefit. People have a name for such a temptation—"messianic complex!"

Our skills and hopes, divinely given, can raise us up for a great letdown! When results come too slowly, we are tempted either to rush ahead or to grumble. Yet, if we place our faith in Jesus whom God raised from the dead, we will not be put to shame. We must confess that Jesus is Lord. Our disappointments will enable us to share in the death of Jesus, our long periods of waiting will establish Jesus' lordship in our hearts. Our confessing with the lips will lead others (not force them) to join prayerfully with us in our faith.

We will be led out of "Egypt," the name for oppression in the Bible. We will be freed of our false ambitions. God's great signs and wonders will be accomplished *by the spirit within us*. The first fruits which we offer will be the fruits of the Spirit within us described by St. Paul: "love, joy, peace, patience, endurance, kindness, generosity, faith, mildness and chastity" (Gal 5:22).

> You who dwell in the shelter of the Most High,
>   Who abide in the shadow of the
>   Almighty
> Say to the Lord, "My refuge and my fortress,
>   my God in whom I trust."

Second Sunday of Lent— "C" Cycle

Gen 15:5-12, 17-18. By a covenant God renewed the promise to Abram (Abraham) of many descendants and their own land.

Phil 3:17-4:1. We eagerly await the coming of our savior, the Lord Jesus Christ, who will then give a new form to our lowly body.

Luke 9:28-36. At Jesus' transfiguration, Moses and Elijah appear and speak with him of his "exodus".

All three Bible readings emphasize hope. Hope constitutes the major driving force of life. Anyone, especially a sick person, who loses the hope or desire for life, quickly disintegrates. The substance of our hope extends beyond our vision, even beyond earthly possibilities. To live here we are obliged to seek the hereafter. Otherwise our present life falls apart! St. Paul sensed this imperative deeply within himself. During one of his captivities, faced with possible death, he wrote:

> I give no thought to what lies behind but
> push on to what is ahead. My entire
> attention is on the finish line as I
> run towards the prize to which God
> calls me—life on high in Christ Jesus.
> (Phil 3:13-14)

These words of St. Paul immediately precede those of the second reading for today.

Abraham, as St. Paul also writes, "hoped against hope" (Rom 4:18). It was difficult to continue trusting in God's promises. It seemed as though a foster child, not a son born to his wife Sarah, would inherit Abraham's name, property and promises. In a mystic sleep Abraham saw God symbolically pass between the sacrificial animals in the form of a flaming torch. The blood flowing between the divided animals represented the one life uniting God and Abraham. The "flaming torch" expressed the wonder and mystery of God's promises and Abraham's hopes at the center of this one life between them.

Abraham's great hope prompts a study in contrast, which St. Paul describes very well. A first group whose "god is their belly and their glory is in their shame," is composed of those persons who decide to live it up today because "tomorrow we die" (Is 22:13). Without hope in their future they seem to have no other alternative than these short flings. People of faith, however, "eagerly await the coming of our savior, the Lord Jesus Christ." Each smallest action acquires extraordinary worth, for its effect will endure forever. Moreover, one's hopes add depth and security to the performance of daily routine.

With Jesus' transfiguration hopes break the bonds of the present moment. Heavenly glory exudes from within and casts a garment of dazzling whiteness about Jesus. Jesus must have been bearing this divine glory always within himself, for such wonder to break loose unexpectedly as this. To live with such godly hopes, ideals and expectations, day by day, is bound to cause tension and frustration, far greater than Abraham's. Yet, by such mystic experience Jesus was convinced that the future belonged to him. It was already present, and this realization could transform evil tension into good excitement!

At each eucharistic celebration we no longer "eagerly await the coming of our Savior, the Lord Jesus

Christ." He is present. "This is my body . . . my blood."
We live for a moment the charity and bliss of heaven.
Strangers sit together at the one banquet table and
partake of the one bread and the one cup. People who
avoid one another in daily life, now eat and drink together. The Eucharist also transforms such ordinary
elements as bread and wine into the body and blood of
Jesus. Everywhere we hear that sacred name, "Jesus!"

During the transfiguration Jesus spoke of his
exodus as the Greek word has it, with Moses and Elijah.
It is correctly translated "passage" in the *New Ameri-
can Bible*. Hopes as beautiful as those of one table of the
Lord shared equally with everyone (1 Cor 10:21;
11:17-22), tell us how far behind we are in our daily
neighborhood and work. We are still in the exodus or
passage towards the fulfillment of these hopes. The
Eucharist raises problems, for it challenges our divi-
sions and prejudices; but it also gives the strength to
work towards the fulfillment. It provides the stamina to
"eagerly await the coming of our Savior." Jesus is
bound to come forever for he has come now at this
moment.

Jesus' *exodus* or passage included his violent death
on the cross. We must all follow this passage. St. Paul
calls upon us to be friends, not "enemies of the cross of
Christ." We are bound to suffer for our hopes, especially
when their fulfillment becomes ever more distant as in
the case of Abraham. Abraham did beget a son in his old
age. Yet, this son Isaac was an only child who like
Abraham never possessed the promised land as his very
own. These unfulfilled hopes can be very frustrating
and can lead us through a passage of fear and suffering.
They also provide us with one of the most glorious of all
opportunities—to hand on to the next generation the

holiest of hopes, the finest drive for life, a promise of life forever in the bonds of charity and peace.

> The Lord is my light and my salvation
> whom should I fear?
> The Lord is my life's refuge;
> of whom should I be afraid?
> Your presence, O Lord, I seek.

Third Sunday of Lent—"C" Cycle

Ex 3:1-8, 13-15. God calls Moses and reveals his sacred name, Yahweh or Lord, from the burning bush.

1 Cor 10:1-6, 10-12. The exodus of Israel out of Egypt, through the desert, toward the Promised Land, "happened . . . as an example . . . [and] a warning to us, upon whom the end of the ages has come."

Luke 13:1-9. The mystery of human events and the patience of God are typified in the fig tree.

"All Scripture" we are told in the second letter to Timothy, "is useful for teaching . . . and training in holiness" (2 Tim 3:16); but today's selections remind us of attitudes more important than usual. In fact, in the second reading Paul is quite conscious of this fact, twice he states: the things in the Bible happened as an example for us. The lesson of some gospel events, however, is too mysterious for our comprehension, certainly too overwhelming for such simplistic explanation as: "The one who suffers more has sinned more!" Likewise in the parable of the fig tree Jesus advises us to be as patient as his heavenly Father is patient, waiting for the mystery of life and its hopes to unravel with good fruit.

In this waiting upon God's revelation or explanation, we experience wondrous events. St. Paul describes them as being "under the cloud" of God's wonderful direction and passing "through the sea" of extraordinary deliverance. Yet, the desert stretch can become unbearably long, its dryness beyond our patience, and so we forget about the "cloud" and the "sea." We begin to "grumble as some of them did" in the days of Moses. "There is an appointed time for everything . . . a time to weep and a time to laugh," a time to be very active and aggressive and a time to be patient and wait in the face of mystery. (*cf.*, Eccles 3:1-11)

The story of Moses' call in the first reading to lead the people out of Egypt to the Promised Land insists that our earliest ideals give direction for a lifetime and abide with us even beyond our death. Moses was convinced that God was summoning him to "rescue [my people] . . . from the hands of the Egyptians and lead them into a good and spacious land, a land flowing with milk and honey." Such a vocation might have been fearful and overpowering enough, if only one-third were asked of Moses—to deliver Israel from Egyptian slavery *or* to lead them through the Sinai desert *or* to bring them across the Jordan into the Promised Land. In fact, it was too much, and Moses died with only two-thirds of it accomplished, and the final one-third, the goal and purpose of it all, left for the next generation.

Faced with unfulfilled hopes, we see the necessity of "waiting"upon the Lord. The Bible frequently calls us to this fundamental virtue. Faced with discouragement and weariness, the prophet Isaiah concluded: "Those who hope in the Lord will renew their strength" (Is 40:31). Hope is identical with the virtue of waiting, except that it adds a quality of optimism.

Elsewhere in the book of Isaiah occurs the classic statement somewhat in the form of a dialogue: What we are expected to do, God is already doing.

> For thus says the Lord God . . .
> By waiting and by calm you shall be saved,
>> in quiet and in trust your strength
>> lies. . . .
> The Lord is waiting to show you favor
>> and he rises to pity you;
> For the Lord is a God of justice·
>> blessed are all who wait for him.
>> (Is 30:15, 18)

"Waiting" can be dangerous, especially when a person like Moses must wait for all his adult years and then be told at the end: there across the Jordan "is the land which I swore to . . . give your people. . . . Feast your eyes upon it, but you shall not cross over" (Deut 34:4). Many other persons would have died frustrated, or more probably they would have given up long ahead of time. The fire in the burning bush would have consumed the scrub bush; the hopes would have burnt out all the surviving energy. Such people then settle for a vocation that is easier, possible of fulfillment on their own terms. Moses, however, rejected any such compromise.

To Moses, then, God revealed his own sacred name, "Yahweh" in Hebrew, "Lord" in English. The Hebrew word in one way reflects Moses' own interior attitude; and in another way it is a response to Moses. "Yahweh" means "He who is always there—I am the one who I am always with you." Spoken by Moses it is a prayer: "Lord be with me"; spoken by the Lord it is a promise: "I will be always there." The name, however, never fully reveals God nor does it describe with any detail what God will do for his people. It is mostly a promise—I will be always there with you.

> Merciful and gracious is the Lord.
>> slow to anger and abounding in
>> kindness.

Fourth Sunday of Lent—"C" Cycle

Josh 5:9a, 10-12. The feast of Passover is celebrated on the plains of Jericho. The Israelites eat the produce of the Promised Land, and the manna ceases.

2 Cor 5:17-21. "The old order has passed away; now all is new." Christ who never sinned became "sin" that we might become the very holiness of God.

Luke 15:1-3, 11-32. The parable of the prodigal father, freely forgiving the younger son.

Within the first reading from *Joshua* the thought moves from an extraordinary event to the remembrance of it, from miracles to a more normal work-a-day existence, from God's providing the miraculous food of manna to the necessity of growing, harvesting and preparing the unleavened cakes and parched grain. The great miracles of the older generation now belong to history; times have changed.

Yet, Israel must never forget those giants of history, her ancestors. The wondrous acts of God, delivering the Hebrew slaves from Egypt, caring for them in the desert, bringing them across the Jordan river, must never be forgotten. And so Israel celebrated her great holydays, particularly the feast of Passover.

"Christ" wrote St. Paul, is "our Passover" (1 Cor 5:7). With "love which surpasses all knowledge" (Eph 3:19) and is "strong as death" (Song 6:6b), Christ became incarnate in our midst, so much a part of "our weakness" that he "was tempted in every way that we are, yet never sinned" (Hebr 4:15). So thoroughly did Jesus plunge into the human side of our life, that he "who did not know sin [appeared] to be sin, so that in him we might become the very holiness of God." With Jesus thus completely a part of our human existence, he appeared weighted down by our sin and we have been able to rise above all sin through his holiness! Because all of us have experienced the presence of Jesus, have been delivered from the slavery of our sin and have been led into the Promised Land of our Church, we celebrate! We commemorate these wonderful, redemptive acts, not just of our ancestors but also within our own, remembered existence.

The second reading brings out the consequences of this, our Passover. "If anyone is in Christ, that person is a new creation. The old order has passed away; now all is new!. . . God, in Christ, was reconciling *the world* to himself, not counting people's transgressions against them. . . . He has entrusted the message of reconciliation to us. That makes us ambassadors for Christ; God as it were appealing through us." These words are as stern as they are beautiful. Such is always the strength of love. For us to be ambassadors of reconciliation of the world to God, we ourselves must be reconciled with everyone in our world! We must be so united with our neighbor—as Christ is united to us—that we take on their weakness and even their sins. By loving forgiveness we transform this sinful situation into the "very holiness of God."

"But who is my neighbor?" Jesus had answered this question in the parable of the Good Samaritan (Luke 10:29-37). In today's gospel the focus is narrowed to a more specific inquiry, "Who is the neighbor whom I must forgive and be reconciled with?" Jesus makes the case as difficult as possible. The neighbor turns out to be the spendthrift brother, who brazenly demanded his inheritance long in advance, immediately abandoned parents and home, and then, as the elder brother reminded the father, "returns after having gone through your wealth with loose women." The most difficult of reconciliations is always between relatives who have been split apart by money, scandal and wasteful living. Civil wars are always the bloodiest with the deepest scars.

Like the prodigal father, we are to be daily on the lookout for the return of these persons whom we deservedly condemn for their sins and find incompatible. God "has entrusted the message of reconciliation to us. *This* makes us ambassadors for Christ, God as it were appealing through us."

In this real way we celebrate the Passover. We share the good fruit of our Promised Land with our neighbor. It was said earlier in this meditation that miracles ceased and the work-a-day existence got under way. Forgiveness of enemies is the greatest miracle of all. Such love will also evoke other miracles, curing the sick, giving sight to the blind, speech and hearing to the deaf mutes, strong limbs to the paralyzed.

> Taste and see the goodness of the Lord!
> When the afflicted person cried out, the Lord heard,
>> and from all his distress he saved him.

Fifth Sunday of Lent — "C" Cycle

Is 43:16-21. See, I am doing something new; opening a
new way through the mighty waters.

Phil 3:8-14. I push on to what is ahead — to know the
power of his resurrection, to share in his sufferings
and to arrive at resurrection from the dead.

John 8:1-11. Jesus forgives the adulterous woman.
Everyone sins and all have need of forgiveness.

Today is the Sunday of new beginning. Even
though we are approaching the end of Lent and the
Good Friday death of Jesus, still we look forward to a
new beginning when we will celebrate the Easter resurrection.

In Isaiah 43 we contemplate the exuberance and
new beginning of *youth*. When old folks were young,
they used to say what the young are still saying today:

> Remember not the events of the past,
>   the things of long ago consider not;
> See, I am doing something new!
>   Now it springs forth, do you not
>   perceive it?

With the optimism of youth, wild animals will be tamed,
water will be found in the desert for the people whom I
form for myself. As a new family, says youth, a way will
open in the sea and a path in the mighty waters.

When St. Paul wrote the epistle to the Philippians,
he was confined to prison and could be facing death or at
least the end of his apostolate. His words proclaim the
new beginnings of a person near death.

> I am racing to grasp the prize . . .
> I give no thought to what lies behind . . .

My entire attention is on the finish line . . .
life on high in Christ Jesus.

These words of St. Paul ring all the more significantly
when they are heard against the setting of earlier words:
"I have come to rate all as loss in the light of the
surpassing knowledge of my Lord Jesus Christ. . . . I
have accounted all else rubbish so that Christ may be
my wealth and I may be in him, not having any justice of
my own." How unbelievable for an old person to be so
young. What more gracious way to grow old?

The gospel selection announces the new beginning
of a sinful person. The cards are stacked against the
adulterous woman, hopelessly according to the doctors
of the law. "This woman whom they force to stand
publicly before Jesus and all the people in the temple
area," has been caught, they triumphantly announce,
"in adultery." She is not only apprehended in the crimi-
nal act, but the law clearly stipulates that "both the
adulterer and the adulteress shall be put to death" (Lev
20:10). Even Deuteronomy, whose legal procedure
tends to be more compassionate, calls for death (Deut
22:22).

Jesus, too, is caught between his own rule of forgiveness and Moses' law of death, between his popular-
ity with the crowd who understand the weakness of the
flesh and his standing with the religious authorities who
rigidly hold to the law. Only goodness as pure as Jesus'
could have untied this Gordian knot. He did it so simply: "Let the man among you who has no sin be the first
to cast a stone at her."

In each of these new beginnings the person could
have taken another route and responded very differently. When the prophet Isaiah comforted his people
during the Babylonian exile, telling them to "hope in the

Lord . . . [and so] renew their strength," (Is 40:31), to "remember not the things of the past" but expect a new and more glorious exodus out of oppression than that of Moses' day, they could have bitterly replied: "we cannot help but remember the past, its agony and destruction, our exile and separations which the Lord inflicted upon us. We will trust now in the Babylonian religion of politics and pleasure." We today are tempted to forget God and put our confidence in business, wealth, clout, prestige, and other such means.

When Paul was faced with death, instead of looking towards a new beginning, the goal of his heavenly call in Christ Jesus, he could have taken the route of self-pity and bitterness. He could have made an appeal to his accomplishments and justice. How many of us can respond this graciously when everything has turned against us and no earthly hope remains, when our own blood relatives have worked to our destruction?

The woman who was caught could also have reacted differently and took the way of blaming others. Where was the man? Has every other adulteress been put to death? We, too, can be tempted to drag up the past of others and excuse ourselves by reciting their sins.

In order to avoid these false decisions and to make our new beginning, we must turn to Jesus as the center of our lives, Jesus who forgives when all the world condemns, who renews when all seems destroyed, who begins new life by rising from the dead.

> The Lord has done great things for us;
> We are filled with joy.
>
> Those that sow in tears
> shall reap rejoicing.

Passion or Palm Sunday—Sixth Sunday of Lent—"C" Cycle

Luke 19:28-40. (Gospel for the Procession). Luke's account of Jesus' messianic entry into Jerusalem heightens the struggle which Jesus will face in the city and temple, and announces the final destruction of the holy city, especially in the fuller account in Luke 19:28-48.

Is 50:4-7. In the prophecy of Isaiah the third Song of the Suffering Servant combines attentive listening and abject humiliation with dignified strength.

Phil 2:6-11. Jesus emptied himself of his divine dignity, to be incarnated in our midst and suffer the humiliation of the cross, as a way to glory and divine exaltation.

Luke 22:14-23:56. The Passion according to Luke portrays Jesus more frequently than the other gospels in prayer, in forgiveness, in concern for others and attracting them to follow, even to take up his cross like Simon of Cyrene.

In doing our best and becoming exhausted in the process, we sense that God wants still more of us. As we surrender to these divine ideals we can be transformed into a person far beyond our human possibilities. Such is the cycle of life-death-life, stressed by St. Luke.

At Palm Sunday Jesus seems to have arrived at the fulfillment of his mission; he is acclaimed triumphantly as Messiah by "the entire crowd of disciples who began to rejoice and praise God loudly for the display of power they had seen." It is possible that as peace and glory resound in the highest, even the angelic choirs are joining. Likewise, the Suffering Servant in the prophecy of

Isaiah has completed his long period of preparation. He has now "a well trained tongue" (in the Hebrew, a tongue which has listened intently before it attempts to speak); he possesses a heart sensitive to others and able to rouse the oppressed and neglected. Yet, the Servant helps others by listening, morning after morning, to God's will in prayer, to other's needs in kindly concern.

When the Suffering Servant and Jesus were best prepared, God asked each of them to suffer rejection and martyrdom. Their best was to be handed over freely, so that they will be consecrated not just in their accomplishments but in their deepest self. In fact, only by the collapse of their achievements and the silencing of their skills will all the world be impressed with the extraordinary depths and strength and purity of their consecration to God.

Jesus had already undergone such a process of giving up everything. Although he had been God, equal in glory and dignity with the Father and the Spirit for all eternity, "he emptied himself and took the form of a slave." Now that he had achieved full adult status, with notable human success, he was asked to give up everything once more—to accept death, even "death on a cross!"

Even though death sweeps upon Jesus with the swift violence of a lion, still Jesus retains a peaceful attitude, quietly and sensitively responding to each new moment of sorrow. Even during the solemn procession towards Jerusalem in Luke's account, Jesus "coming within sight of the city, . . . wept over it and said: 'If only you had known the path to peace this day.' " Throughout the Passion narrative Jesus appears as a person absorbed in prayer towards his heavenly Father, attentive to the least needs of those around him. He "turned around and looked at Peter," who had just denied Jesus three times, "and Peter remembered the word [of] . . . the Lord . . ., went out and wept bitterly." What tender, strong, forgiving love must have been communicated in that "look" of Jesus towards Peter.

Jesus beseeched the women who lamented his agonizing way of the cross: "Do not weep for me. Weep for yourselves and for your children." He prayed that forgiveness be graciously shown his executioners, as nails tore through his body. He forgave the thief, and his last words were the peaceful prayer: "Father, unto your hands I commend my spirit."

We learn from the Suffering Servant and from Jesus that our greatest triumph lies more in who we are than in what we do, in how we respond to others than in how they treat us, in our consistent attitude of prayer and forgiveness, rather than in their flattery and betrayal. We are given an opportunity to be ever more thoroughly ourselves, if we can remain rooted in God during all the passing, changing seasons of life. We will learn this depth of ourselves, only if we are emptied. We will gauge our strength and worth, not by surface accomplishments but rather by the profound motivation beneath. We must arrive at total absorption in God before we will confess with all our being that God is the source, the way and the goal of life.

Jesus shows us, moreover, that this awareness of God's presence must include a sensitivity to all God's people at all moments of life. Then our triumph is complete in God and through God. When the peace and glory in the highest will be deeply rooted on earth, Jesus will be glorified as Lord—in us and with the Father and the Spirit.

My God, my God, why have you abandoned
    me?
You, O Lord, be not far from me;
    O my help, hasten to aid me.

PART THREE

Easter

Rom 6:3-11. Through baptism we die with Christ and rise to a new life in Him, freed from sin, no longer slaves.

Matt 28:1-10. (Year A) Jesus' resurrection is announced by earthquakes, angelic visitations and the wondrous vision of Jesus Himself. The disciples are to go to Galilee where Jesus will visit them.

Mark 16:1-8. (Year B) The women come despondently to the tomb in order to anoint Jesus; on seeing the tomb empty and hearing the young man's words, they "fled from the tomb bewildered . . . and said nothing to anyone."

Luke 24:1-12. (Year C) The women are bringing spices to the tomb and find it empty. Two men speak of Jesus' resurrection. To the women's message, the other disciples later react with disbelief or amazement.

Lent may have seemed an exceptionally long stretch of prayer and fasting, intensified by the agony of Good Friday and left incomplete with the darkness and silent sorrow of the extended Easter Vigil service. Suddenly, this night Lent stops, the *Gloria* rings out, the bells fill the air with vibrant excitement, and we are stunned, as the opening prayer declares, by "the radiance of the risen Christ."

Such a quick and dramatic change brings as many different reactions as there are disciples of Christ and people in church. The three gospels of Matthew, Mark and Luke all seem to go their own way in the resurrection accounts. The variations are noticeable at once. Most striking of all, perhaps, is the wide range of personal responses. "The guards grew paralyzed with fear." The women were frightened, half-overjoyed, half fearful, on the run! And Jesus says so quietly, "Peace!" In Mark's gospel the women fled bewildered and trembling . . . [and] said nothing to anyone." Luke, similar to the other evangelists, gives the place of honor and faith to women, who are "terrified" at first but almost immediately are the first preachers of the resurrection, even to the eleven apostles. These latter, however, considered the story "nonsense" at first!

Evidently, happiness and holiness can be "too good to be true." We can spoil the finest moments of joy in ourselves and in others by our lack of faith in the goodness and generosity in others. We suspect that it is all a show or make-belief. We may doubt the motives, why others appear kind to us. We hesitate to reassure others in their efforts to improve themselves and to grow in their talents and hopes. We can destroy hopes and throw a dark mantle of gloom and fear over the future!

Easter delcares that great reversals are not only possible. They actually happen. Miracles can and do break the monotony of daily human existence—*if we believe*. We need also to be humble and open to change, particularly change in the lives of the poor and oppressed.

We must develop a bond of loving concern with the underprivileged and with worried and fearful hearts. We should feel the ache of hunger and wandered with the lonely in their darkness. With the women of Jesus' day, we cannot separate ourselves from those we love, even in their death and burial, as we return to the tomb. Lent should have developed such a loving union with the needy, the distressed and the "dead" that our hearts are one with them.

We are ready for the earthquake. God who loves even more than we are capable of loving, cannot endure it any longer! Jesus must rise from the dead—*today*. Such a sudden transformation—of conversion, health, hope fulfilled, new visions and messages for the future—leaves us baffled. The light and the reality are so magnificent, that we can be at peace only if we believe—believe in Jesus, in ourselves and in all our brothers and sisters.

> Through baptism into his death we were buried with him, so that, just as Christ was raised from the dead by the glory of the Father, we too might live a new life. Alleluia. Alleluia. Alleluia.

Easter Sunday

Acts 10:34, 37-43. The apostles are personal witnesses that Jesus rose from the dead, for they "ate and drank with him." They are commissioned to preach Jesus, to whom the prophets testify and through whom there is forgiveness of sin.

Col 3:1-4. "Your life is hidden now with Christ in God."

1 Cor 5:6-8. (Alternate Second Reading) The risen Christ is the unleavened bread of sincerity and truth by which we rise from the dead.

John 20:1-9. (Morning Mass) Mary Magdalene, Peter and John all arrive at the tomb, one with wonder, the others at first with perplexity, all eventually with faith that Jesus is risen.

Luke 24:13-35. (Evening Mass) On Easter the three disciples on their way to Emmaus recognize Jesus in the breaking of bread.

Jesus' resurrection proclaims the miraculous transformation of our earthly existence. We remain as we are, men and women with earthly bodies; Jesus too for all eternity will be the son of Mary who was nurtured by the love and nourishment of his home in Nazareth. The miracle of his resurrection happened right here in the midst of his relatives, disciples and friends. We can sense Peter's excitement as he pours out the words: we "ate and drank with him after he rose from the dead." The apostle Thomas had even placed his finger into the scar of the nails in Jesus' hands. It really happened! This apparition is not an eerie ghost but the real Jesus!

Even though the events took place at a particular place and at an unique point of time on planet earth, still the disciples' lives were transformed into some kind of heavenly existence. True, at first they all reacted differently—with wonder, perplexity, bewilderment, or even unbelief. Eventually, all were caught up in the wave of excitement: Jesus is risen and we are witnesses! Nonetheless, the morning gospel ends with the baffling statement: "they did not understand the Scriptures that Jesus had to rise from the dead."

The apostles evidently had so much more to learn and especially to appreciate about Jesus of Nazareth. Not only at Pentecost but continuously during the days, months, and years after Pentecost, Jesus' disciples would be illumined by the Holy Spirit. They would recognize ever more and more the power of Jesus' resurrection in their daily lives.

We too believe that Jesus has risen from the dead—theoretically, at least—yet we all have to be enlightened and strengthened by the Holy Spirit. We need that practical wisdom to recognize the power of the risen Jesus in one another. Real faith in Jesus' resurrection perceives that *all of us* "have been raised up in company with Christ."

We are placed upon earth and yet we are expected to live a heavenly existence here. We are to manifest the fruits or gifts of the spirit as St. Paul describes them in the same Epistle to the Colossians: "heartfelt mercy, kindness, humility, meekness and patience. Bear with one another. . . . Forgive as the Lord has forgiven you. Over all these virtues put on love. . . . Christ's peace must reign in your hearts" (Col 3:13-15).

While these qualities may seem to be passive and without effort, we will all admit, in our honest moment, that the greatest effort is expended in forgiving and in being patient. The spirit with which we summon all of our power to respond with love and peace will be the manifestation of Jesus' resurrection. As we live with such an attitude, the prophecies will be fulfilled in us. By eating and drinking with us, by living familiarly in our everyday life, people will sense the full meaning of Jesus' resurrection.

> This is the day the Lord has made;
> let us rejoice and be glad.

BIBLICAL INDEX

(Asterisk indicates a more extended reflection.)

157

TOPICAL INDEX